Move to Learn

INTEGRATING MOVEMENT INTO THE EARLY CHILDHOOD CURRICULUM

Joye Newman, MA, and Miriam P. Feinberg, PhD

ACKNOWLEDGMENTS

We are extremely appreciative of all the help we received while writing this book. We're particularly grateful to early childhood educators Sheri Brown, Stephanie Slater, Shelley Remer, Talma Brener Epstein, and Leslie Slan for their invaluable suggestions and support.

Thanks to the Gryphon House team, including Stephanie Roselli, editor extraordinaire, Terrey Hatcher, and Rosanna Mollett.

We learned so much from many delightful children and their creative and devoted teachers whose classrooms we were privileged to visit.

We are blessed with admiration and encouragement from our wonderful family members.

BULK PURCHASE

Gryphon House books are available for special premiums and sales promotions as well as for fund-raising use. Special editions or book excerpts also can be created to specifications. For details, contact the director of marketing at Gryphon House.

DISCLAIMER

Gryphon House, Inc., cannot be held responsible for damage, mishap, or injury incurred during the use of or because of activities in this book. Appropriate and reasonable caution and adult supervision of children involved in activities and corresponding to the age and capability of each child involved are recommended at all times. Do not leave children unattended at any time. Observe safety and caution at all times.

Move to Learn

Integrating
Movement
into the Early
Childhood
Curriculum

**Joye Newman, MA, and
Miriam P. Feinberg, PhD**

Gryphon House

Lewisville, NC

COPYRIGHT

©2015 Joye Newman and Miriam P. Feinberg

Published by Gryphon House, Inc.

P. O. Box 10, Lewisville, NC 27023

800.638.0928; 877.638.7576 (fax)

Visit us on the web at www.gryphonhouse.com.

Some interior photographs courtesy of Shutterstock Photography, www.shutterstock.com.

LIBRARY OF CONGRESS CATALOGING-IN-PUBLICATION DATA

The Cataloging-in-Publication Data is registered with the Library of Congress for ISBN: 978-0-87659-560-2.

Table of Contents

FOREWORD

Movement is a language, a way we communicate with the world. It is one of the first forms of communication children use. The baby who turns his head toward the sound of his mother's voice, the arched back that says no, and the burrowing snuggle that communicates contentment—these are all clear movement messages to a parent. As children grow, they use movement to express a need or a feeling. A caregiver can tell by an ear pull that a child is tired or by the reach for the bottle that the child is hungry. Somehow, we know what each of these movements mean, and we respond with our own movements and add the words to narrate the exchange. We "read" children by their movement language and respond sometimes without even realizing it. The first wave, the first steps, and the first blown kiss all mark a way of communicating that occurs long before spoken language develops.

By the preschool years, children are delighting in learning the language of moving their bodies in new ways. They are thrilled when they learn to snap their fingers or hop on one foot. Conquering the slide and monkey bars is a way of saying, "I am growing up!" As children learn more and more complex movements, they incorporate them into their lives. A spontaneous dance can express a multitude of feelings. A simple facial expression can speak a thousand words.

The sense of mastery that comes from motor skills provides a foundation for all other skills. After conquering walking and climbing, children are ready to play with the way they move. Children are fascinated by how objects and animals move. Have you ever watched a child imitate the movement of an animal or pretend to be an airplane? The freely expressed movement is often much better than what we could instruct them to do. They use many skills at the same time to express what they observe and construct their own knowledge about the world around them.

When we provide children with movement activities, we not only enrich their motor, cognitive, and social skills, but we also expand their movement vocabulary. They learn to listen to their bodies and express themselves with creativity and awareness. This expanded vocabulary of movements is similar to learning new "big words"—and we all know how much they love that! The oft-heard phrase of "Look what I can do!" is a celebration of these skills. We are so fortunate to have the ability to inspire children to use their bodies as a learning and expressive tool. May all children benefit from the brilliant ideas shared in this book.

—Ellen Booth Church

Introduction

Human beings are born to move. In fact, we begin to move at the moment of conception and continue moving as long as we are healthy and capable. Movement is innate and fundamental to life. When we imagine happy young children, we picture exuberant and unbridled movement. This is not only natural but also necessary for optimal physical, cognitive, emotional, and social development.

With the advent of technology, many of us find that our lifestyles have become more sedentary. We often introduce computers and other technology to children at a very early age, sometimes even before they are physiologically prepared to master those skills. As early childhood educators, we are responsible for preparing children to handle the world in which they live. In many cases, this includes the ability to work with keyboards and screens. At the same time, we know that movement lays the framework upon which all future skills are built. It is, therefore, imperative that movement be a primary element in the early childhood curriculum.

It is imperative that movement be a primary element in the early childhood curriculum.

With an awareness of the profound impact movement makes on the developing child, we look for ways to bring movement to all elements of the school curriculum. We believe that movement is an essential part of living and growing and should be encouraged and embraced at all times of the day. The clear way to present both movement and cognitive materials successfully is through an integrated curriculum, with cognitive and motor activities presented as one, thus encouraging children's learning and creativity in all areas.

The Importance of Movement

Those who feel comfortable in their bodies are often more competent and seem to find life easier than those who are less at ease physically. As adults, we have an incredibly large repertoire of movements that we take for granted. For instance, when driving a car, one automatically lifts the directional indicator handle to signal a right turn. Imagine being in a car where the signals are reversed. One would need to think every time a turn is required, making driving much more difficult. From the time of birth, each new experience creates neural pathways that grow and are strengthened by further movement. As these movements become automatic, the brain has greater capacity to focus on new information.

In the past, children had a variety of movement opportunities from their earliest ages. Those movement experiences built a foundation for the development of sensory, visual, and perceptual motor skills, allowing children to concentrate on learning. Today, parents and educators frequently offer electronic gadgets and videos in the hope of teaching new skills, without realizing that those practices deprive children of opportunities for physical activities and human interaction:

○ Manipulating an avatar on a screen does not provide the sensory, perceptual, or visual-motor input that is generated from actual physical experiences. For instance, rolling down a hill sends information to the middle ear about gravity and gives information through the skin concerning touch. Both of these messages become essential when the child learns to write but are not attainable when interacting with an avatar.

○ A child who interacts with a game pad is limited in his field of vision. Concentrating only on the electronic instrument in front of him deprives him of the opportunity to alternate between looking far away and close-up. Alternating the distance of visual focus, necessary for copying from the board when in school, is developed when a child throws and catches a ball with a partner.

○ "Moving" through a two-dimensional world is quite different from actually moving through space. The spatial awareness that a child acquires by moving herself forward and backward, sideways and diagonally builds skills needed to organize her paper, her desk, her thoughts, and her body.

Scientists now recognize that stimulation through movement and sensory experiences during the early childhood years is necessary for the development of the mature brain. Research has shown that cognitive development and motor development may be fundamentally interrelated. The period for the development of basic gross-motor skills appears to be most available from the prenatal period to around age five. It is clear that teachers who provide experiences (including motor activities) engaging all areas of the cortex can anticipate deeper learning than if they engage fewer areas.

Children from birth to age six are developing the foundation for who they will become for the rest of their lives. While we can teach them information, we cannot teach skills that they learn only by moving. It is our responsibility as preschool educators to promote movement opportunities through an environment rich in sensory, perceptual, and visual-motor experiences.

How to Use This Book

This book presents a variety of classroom and outdoor activities in six curriculum areas. As you use it, you will notice that ideas presented in the integrated curriculum areas often overlap. For instance, "Let's Have Sound Day" on page 23 under Language and Literacy could as appropriately be placed in the Music curriculum category, as could "Dancing with Your Ribbon" on page 52, which is currently found under Mathematics.

In designing these activities, we have been mindful of important aspects of early learning:

○ **Providing preschoolers with numerous sensory-motor experiences**
We emphasize visual-motor activities, including those integrating visual information with fine- and gross-motor movements.

○ **Integrating a variety of gross-motor activities**
The activities involve coordination of movements, postural control, and locomotion such as rolling, jumping, crawling, and creeping.

○ **Combining music with movement**
Adding music to the activities provides additional learning opportunities, enhances the auditory system, and develops the sense of rhythm. Music can be a social activity, eliciting communication in a variety of ways.

○ **Offering directed movement activities to do outdoors**
Even though nondirected playing on the playground is beneficial to young children, directed movement, both indoors and out, is equally important.

○ **Incorporating opportunities for social awareness and self-expression**
The activities are designed to encourage freedom of expression within a wide range of abilities. As there are no right or wrong responses, everyone can succeed at his own level, feeling a sense of accomplishment.

Feel free to use these activities exactly as they are presented or change them to meet the needs of your students. Some of the activities are brief, while others are more involved and might require longer periods of time. We have not included age ranges with the activities, as each classroom is unique in its physical, emotional, and social character.

Wherever possible, we have listed the activities in order of difficulty. Ideas offered can be used as references or as a day-to-day guide, regardless of the number of children in your class, the physical size of your classroom, and the quality and quantity of equipment available to you. The majority of these activities can be modified to include children with a broad range of physical and intellectual challenges. Suggested activities will enhance the learning experiences both in the classroom and also outside, during circle time, with small and large groups, and as one-to-one interactions.

Moving children are developing children. There are many ways that we can help them develop through movement. They can be invited to jump to the line rather than simply walking there when they line up at the door. They can point with their elbows rather than using only words to identify a specific object. They can use body parts requiring movement in ways other than walking when transitioning to a new activity.

While everyone benefits from the inclusion of movement, such activities are **crucial** for young children's development in all areas and should be purposefully integrated into every part of the early childhood curriculum.

Language and Literacy

Literacy, defined as the ability to read and write, is essential for children's success in school and throughout life. Although reading and writing skills continue to develop during one's lifetime, the early years are crucial for the development of literacy. While we do not encourage teaching reading and writing during the preschool years, the seeds of literacy can be planted through literacy-rich experiences.

Prereading

Allocating time to read to children daily encourages their language acquisition as well as their appreciation of literature. Children who are read to regularly are more likely than others to develop listening skills; lengthened attention spans; and the ability to express themselves confidently, easily, and clearly. In addition, they gain new information, ideas, and life skills through literacy activities.

Many children's books provide ample opportunities for movement by asking children to act out the story. In *Goodnight Moon,* for instance, the children can imitate the story characters by skittering like the mouse, moving quietly like the old lady, or making their bodies look like chairs. When reading a book that provides less obvious means for movement, it is still possible to find ways to move, sometimes by inviting suggestions from the children themselves.

Let's Say Good Night

This is a great activity to do just before nap time, when the emphasis is on *quiet*. When you need to get the children moving and grooving, focus on *loud*.

WHAT TO DO:

1. Read *Goodnight Moon* by Margaret Wise Brown to the children. Any children's book that features a quiet mood will work for this activity.

2. Ask the children, "Is *Goodnight Moon* a quiet story or a loud story?" Listen to their responses.

3. Ask the children to stand up and spread out so they have room to move without bumping into each other.

4. Ask, "Can you show me a quiet way to move your arms?" Let them move their arms quietly. As they do, comment on their movements: "Cammie is moving her arms quietly over her head." "LaToya is moving her arms quietly from side to side."

5. Continue the activity, encouraging the children to move different body parts in a quiet way:
   - legs
   - fingers
   - head
   - feet

6. Ask the children to show how they can make noises with their hands. As they do so, comment on their movements: "Taylor is clapping." "Kenny is trying to snap his fingers!"

7. Continue the activity, encouraging the children to make noises with different body parts:
   - feet
   - knees
   - elbows

How Does Snow Look?

This slow-paced activity can be relaxing. For children who are able to move each limb separately, snow angels can be very calming.

WHAT TO DO:

1. Read *The Snowy Day* by Ezra Jack Keats or *Snow* by Uri Shulevitz to the children. Any children's book that features snow will work for this activity.

2. Talk about snow with the children. Ask, "How do snowflakes look when they fall?" "Do they fall fast or slowly?" If you live in an area where snow is a rarity, consider viewing a short video clip of snowfall.

3. Ask the children, "Can you move across the room *very* slowly, just like a slowly moving snowflake?" Encourage the children to move, and comment as they do: "Brenda is slowly turning." "Jerry is slowly stepping."

4. Encourage the children to move slowly in other ways:
   - on tiptoe
   - while sliding on their tummies
   - while walking on their knees
   - while walking backward

5. Ask the children, "What color is snow?" Ask them to look at their shirts. If they have white on their shirts, encourage them to twirl around the circle back to their place like a twirling snowflake.

6. Encourage them to move if they are wearing white:
   - on their shoes—march around the circle and go back to their places.
   - on their pants—slide around the circle and go back to their places.
   - anywhere else—slink around the circle and go back to their places.

7. Tell the children, "When it snows, you can make snow angels by lying in the snow and moving your arms and legs. Peter in *The Snowy Day* makes snow angels with his body." Ask the children to lie on their backs on the floor.

8. Tell them to slide one arm over their heads and then slide that arm back down to their sides. Continue, asking them to focus on different body parts:
   ○ Slide your other arm over your head and then back down to your side.
   ○ Slide both arms over your head and then back down to your two sides.
   ○ Slide one leg out to the side and then back straight down.
   ○ Slide your other leg out to the side and then back straight down.
   ○ Slide both legs out to the side and then back straight down.

The Peddler and His Caps

This activity provides opportunities for pretend and actual practice with developing balance.

Preparation: You will need beanbags for part of this activity, one for each child.

WHAT TO DO:

1. Read *Caps for Sale* by Esphyr Slobodkina.

2. Talk with the children about how the peddler manages to balance the caps on his head. Ask them for their ideas about how he does it.

3. Ask, "Can you move around the room pretending to carry all those caps on your head?" Let the children pretend to balance the caps as they move.

4. Continue the activity, encouraging the children to pretend to carry the caps on different body parts:

   ○ on one hand   ○ on their backs

   ○ on their elbows   ○ on one foot

5. Give each child a beanbag. Ask, "Can you move around the room carrying the beanbag on your head?" Let them try to balance their beanbags as they move.

6. Continue the activity, letting them balance a beanbag on different body parts:

   ○ on one hand   ○ on their back

   ○ on an elbow   ○ on one foot

   Ask the children to put the beanbags in a box or basket when they are finished.

7. Encourage the children to copy you as you move. Say, "Now, I'll be the peddler, and you'll be the monkeys. When I move a certain way, you copy me the way the monkeys copied the peddler." Move around and let the children try to copy you.

Where Should We Go?

Encourage the children to move to any part of the classroom they like as they listen carefully, responding to your movement words. This activity emphasizes the development of spatial relationships and listening skills.

WHAT TO DO:

1. Read *Oh, the Places You'll Go!* by Dr. Seuss to the children. Talk with them about places they would like to go and ways to get there.

2. Tell them that you are going to go all over the classroom. Ask, "Can you look all around the room and find something round (or curvy, square, or red)? Find a way to move to that object without walking to it, such as crawling or hopping."

3. Ask, "As you look around the room, can you see something green? Can you go to that place moving way down low?" Encourage the children to move close to the floor. When they reach their destination, ask them to come back to the circle by moving way up high, perhaps by walking on tiptoe.

4. Continue the activity, asking the children to move in a variety of ways:
   - quietly
   - loudly
   - quickly
   - slowly
   - by yourself
   - with a partner

5. Encourage the children to travel to any spot in the room moving on one hand and two feet.

6. Continue, encouraging the children to travel in a variety of ways:
   - moving on two hands and one foot
   - moving on one hand and one foot
   - moving on two different parts of your body

Prewriting

Well-developed sensory-motor, perceptual-motor, and visual skills are essential for successful writing. These include proprioception—the awareness of sensations coming from muscles and joints. Most children will have the complex skills needed for writing at approximately six years of age. Until then, it is our responsibility as early childhood educators to offer introductory activities that encourage children to practice these skills:

O Proprioception—using a pencil with appropriate pressure (not too much or too little)

O Laterality—holding a paper still with one hand while moving a pencil across the paper with the other hand

O Awareness of directionality and the ability to move body parts in the desired direction

O Easily crossing the midline—moving a hand or eye across the vertical center of the body

Let's Make Cereal Chains

Before children can hold pencils, they need fine-motor control. This activity lets the children practice pincer movements by stringing. Rather than showing the children how to pick up small objects, provide them with materials and the time to practice on their own. The pincer movement will develop naturally.

Preparation: For this activity, each child will need a 6"–8" piece of string. Tie a knot at one end, and dip the other end in a bit of glue to provide a "point." They will also need some round cereal, such as Cheerios. Fill small bowls or cups with the cereal, and set them out on a table for the children.

WHAT TO DO:

1. Ask the children, "Can you take some cereal out of the bowl?"

2. Ask them to pick up the pieces one at a time and place them in a line. Let them practice putting the cereal in a line on the table.

3. Give each child a piece of string. Encourage them to thread the cereal onto the strings.

4. When they are finished with the activity, let them eat their cereal as a snack.

Let's Use Rhythm Sticks

Before a child can write smoothly, she needs to be able to hold her paper still with one hand while moving her other hand to form the letters. This activity lets the children practice moving one hand at a time.

Preparation: Give one set of rhythm sticks to each child.

WHAT TO DO:

1. Ask the children to pass the rhythm sticks around and around their bodies, passing them from one hand to the next. Let them practice the movement.

2. Ask them to try passing the sticks around their bodies in the other direction.

3. Invite the children to hit the floor with both rhythm sticks at the same time.

4. Ask them to hit the floor with one stick at a time.

5. Encourage them to show their own ways to move one stick while keeping the other stick still. Comment on how they are moving their sticks: "Jenna is waving one stick in the air

and holding the other stick still." "Chase is tapping one stick on the floor and holding the other stick still."

I'm Here and There

Before a child can recognize differences in certain letters, such as *b* and *p*, *b* and *d*, and *q* and *p*, he needs an understanding of directionality. One of the best ways to reinforce directionality is to use words and phrases such as *above, below, beside, in front of, behind, over, under, up, down, backward,* and *forward*.

Preparation: Give each child a beanbag.

WHAT TO DO:

1. Ask the children to show you a way to be *in front of* their beanbags. Comment on their choices: "Matthew is sitting in front of his beanbag." "Gracie is standing on one foot in front of her beanbag."

2. Ask them to show a way to be *next to* their beanbags. Comment on their choices.

3. Tell them that you will say a word, and they can listen and figure out where to put their beanbags:
    - *above* you
    - *below* you
    - *beside* you
    - *under* you
    - *over* you

    Comment on their choices.

Follow the Flashlight

Before a child can write fluidly across the page, she needs to be able to track her eyes smoothly from side to side.

Preparation: You will need a flashlight for this activity.

WHAT TO DO:

1. Ask the children to lie down on their backs on the floor. Tell them that you will turn out the lights for this activity.

2. As they lie on the floor in the darkened room, shine a flashlight very slowly on the ceiling. Ask the children to watch the light as it moves.

3. Ask them to hold up a finger and point to the light as it moves.

4. Continue the activity, encouraging them to follow the light with different body parts:
   - one finger from each hand
   - an elbow
   - a foot
   - a chin
   - a tongue
   - another part of the body

Awareness of Sounds

From infancy, children are increasingly aware of the sounds of speech. Making children aware of sounds in their environment, by singing, reciting rhymes, and speaking with them, prepares them for participating in conversations, reading, and writing.

Let's Have Sound Day

Invite the children to decide on a sound for the day, such as the sound of a tambourine, a drum, a rain stick, or a bell. This activity helps develop listening skills and self-control.

Preparation: Have a variety of noisemakers available, such as a bell, a tambourine, and a drum.

WHAT TO DO:

1. Ask the children what sound they would like to choose for the sound of the day. Let them see what their options are. Tell them that the sound they decide upon will be used all day.

2. When they have decided on the sound, ask them to freeze when they hear it. Let them practice moving around the room in various ways, such as jumping, sliding, hopping, and marching, then freezing when they hear the sound of the day. Say, "Remember today's sound. When you hear it, stop what you're doing and listen for directions for our next activity."

3. Each day, let the children choose a sound for that day. Give them opportunities to practice stopping their activities and listening for instructions whenever they hear it.

Making and Listening to Sounds

To be able to differentiate among sounds, children need to be able to visualize the objects making the sounds. Feel free to expand the range of objects used to include materials in the classroom, on the playground, or brought to school by the children.

Preparation: You will need a paper bag for each child. In separate bowls, set out a variety of materials, such as pennies, marbles, feathers, cotton balls, and buttons.

WHAT TO DO:

1. Put some marbles in a paper bag. Ask the children to listen as you shake the bag. Ask, "How does it sound when I shake marbles in the paper bag? Does it sound loud or soft?"

2. Take out the marbles, and put some feathers in the bag. Ask, "How does it sound when I shake feathers in the paper bag? Does it sound loud or soft?" Ask them why they think the two items, marbles and feathers, sound different.

3. Give a paper bag to each child. Provide bowls of rice, pennies, marbles, buttons, cotton balls, and feathers for them to explore. Say, "We'll listen to the sounds that each of these objects make." Try each material, one by one. Talk with the children about the different sounds.

4. Let them make their own shakers using any material they like. As they work, talk with them about the materials they choose and the sounds they hear.

5. Perform a concert using all of their shakers.

What Is That Musical Sound?

This is a fun way to introduce children to instrumental music.

Preparation: You will need a variety of instruments for this activity, such as a triangle, a drum, and a whistle.

WHAT TO DO:

1. Play an instrument, such as a triangle, for the children, and let them listen to the sound it makes. Talk with them about what they hear.

2. Play another instrument, such as a drum, for the children. Talk with them about what they hear.

3. Play a third instrument, such as a whistle, for the children. Talk with them about what they hear.

4. Ask, "Do you notice the differences in the sounds of each of these instruments? How are they different?"

5. Tell them that you are going to play some sounds.
   - Tell them they are to jump when they hear the triangle.
   - When they hear the whistle, they are to spin around.
   - When they hear the drum, they are to sit on their bottoms.

   Let them practice moving in certain ways to certain sounds.

6. Encourage them to move around the room in a variety of ways, such as wiggling, sliding, or walking on tiptoe. Remind them that when they hear one of the instruments, they should do that action: jumping for the triangle, spinning for the whistle, and sitting for the drum. Let them practice moving, listening, and doing certain actions.

Sounds in Our Neighborhood

People of all ages may benefit from learning to appreciate sounds around them. It is never too early to start paying attention.

Preparation: You will need a recording device, such as a small tape recorder or cell phone, for this activity.

WHAT TO DO:

1. Take the children on a walk outside. As you walk, ask the children to listen for the sounds around them. Talk about what they hear.
2. Record the environmental sounds, such as traffic, construction, dogs barking, birds, insects, and footsteps, as you walk. Ask the children, "Who hears a loud sound? Let's record it." "Who hears a quiet sound? Let's record it."
3. Return to the classroom. Play the recorded sounds for the children.
4. As you listen together, ask the children if they can remember what made each sound.

Participating in Conversation

Conversation is the verbal exchange of information, feelings, and thoughts. As children become better listeners, they are more adept at engaging in conversation. Their speaking skills may include the ability to transmit ideas and questions. The teacher's voice can be a very powerful tool, and facial expressions and body language can sometimes create stronger messages than words alone. Use those tools in a variety of ways as you explore ways to communicate with the children.

Listening for the "Magic" Word

Modify this activity as often as you choose by introducing a new "magic" word and corresponding action. We suggest using the same word and action throughout the day.

WHAT TO DO:

1. Tell the children that, together, you will think of a word to use as a "magic" word for the day. Any word, such as *chair*, is appropriate.

2. When they have decided on the word for the day, such as *chair*, tell them that whenever they hear that word, they are to sit down. Ask, "Can you sit down when you hear *chair*?"

3. Let them practice listening for the word and sitting down when they hear it. Say, "Listen with your ears, not with your eyes. I might trick you." Then, just for fun, before saying the word, say *hair*, *deer*, *chart*, or another word that sounds a bit like *chair*.

4. Use sentences throughout the day that feature the "magic" word. Comment on the children's listening skills: "Sara heard the 'magic' word. She is sitting."

Listen Carefully

Children sometimes depend on their visual systems to give them information that is auditory in nature. This activity encourages children to trust what they hear, separating the visual from the auditory.

WHAT TO DO:

1. Tell the children that you are going to challenge them to listen carefully. Say, "Listen carefully, and sit down when I clap my hands."

2. Let the children practice listening for you to clap. Say, "Remember to use your ears, not your eyes." For a fun challenge, pretend to clap sometimes, without actually bringing your hands together to make a noise.

3. Ask, "Did you notice that sometimes I didn't really clap but only pretended to? When I pretend to clap, just stay standing." Let the children practice listening some more.

4. Ask for a volunteer to lead the clapping. Say, "We'll take turns leading the clapping or pretending to clap."

Taking Turns

Young children in group settings benefit from listening to others and having others listen to them. This activity includes visual cues to help the children distinguish the start and finish of each child's turn.

WHAT TO DO:

1. Tell the children that you will play a game in which they need to listen carefully and take turns. To show them how, ask a child, "Jeremy, can you clap your hands over and over for a few seconds? And, Leslie, can you begin clapping when Jeremy finishes clapping? Wait until Jeremy stops clapping before you start." Let the two volunteers practice until the children understand what to do.

2. Tell the children that they will now go around the circle, giving everyone a chance to clap. Start with one child, and encourage each child in turn to listen and clap when the previous child stops clapping.

3. When each child in the circle has had a turn to clap, start clapping again and go around the circle in the other direction.

Let's Play Movement Show and Tell

Replace traditional Show and Tell with this movement-filled version of the game.

WHAT TO DO:

1. Invite the children to show and tell about movements instead of objects. Ask a volunteer to show a movement: "Sophia, would you like to take a turn showing us your movement and telling us about it?"

2. Let the child do a movement and say what she wishes about it.

3. Ask the children, "Can everyone move the way Sophia is moving?"

4. Give each child a turn to move in any way he chooses. Say, "Let's take turns showing our movements and then talking about them."

Phonetics

Phonetics is the branch of linguistics dealing with the sounds of speech and their production. It is the system of speech sounds of a language.

What's Today's Sound?

This activity has nothing to do with letters but everything to do with phonetics. Letter sounds can be confusing for children who are already learning letters.

WHAT TO DO:

1. Tell the children that they are going to choose a sound for the day. Ask, "What should our sound be for today? How about *s-s-s*?" Emphasize the sound rather than the letter.

2. Ask them to move in a way that starts with the *s-s-s* sound. For example, ask, "Can we *stomp* all around the room?" Comment as the children move: "Van is stomping. *Stomping* has a *s-s-s* sound." Ask the children for other suggestions.

3. Tell them, "We'll use the *s-s-s* sound all day. We'll sit at the table later and eat strawberries and celery." Emphasize the *s-s-s* sound in those words and in other words you use throughout the day "Sandi's name has an *s-s-s* sound." "James said *sand*. *Sand* has an *s-s-s* sound."

Whose Name Am I Thinking Of?

By emphasizing beginning sounds of words, children develop awareness of those sounds.

WHAT TO DO:

1. Tell the children that you are going to think about the /d/ sound. Ask, "Can you jump three times if you have a name beginning with the /d/ sound?" Comment on the children who jump: "David is jumping. *David* starts with a /d/ sound." "Devonia is jumping. *Devonia* starts with a /d/ sound."

2. Choose another sound to think about. Ask, "Can you think of someone in this circle whose name starts with a /p/ sound?" Say, "If you can think of someone whose name starts with /p/, point to that person using your elbows." Comment on the children's actions: "David is pointing to Peter. *Peter* starts with a /p/ sound." Continue the game, asking the children to point using different body parts:

    ○ nose

    ○ foot

    ○ knee

3. Tell the children to jump three times, and then choose a different sound.

Let's Play I Spy

Children can learn new words and concepts from each other by playing games such as I Spy.

WHAT TO DO:

1. Ask the children to guess what you see. "Who can tell me what I spy? It starts with the /t/ sound." Emphasize the sound rather than the letter.

2. Let the children guess things in the room that have a /t/ sound. Comment on their choices and offer clues: "Erin says *table* has a /t/ sound. Yes, it does—she's correct. But, I see something else that has a /t/ sound. Can you see something that we play with that starts with a /t/ sound? Yes! Justin guessed it: the tambourine."

3. Encourage the children to look for anything in the room that starts with the /t/ sound. Say, "Jump to something that starts with /t/." Comment on their choices: "Nancy jumped over to Terrey. Yes, *Terrey* starts with a /t/ sound."

4. Encourage them to move in different ways to objects that start with different sounds: "Now, twirl to something that starts with a /d/ sound." "Hop to something that starts with an /m/ sound."

Let's Count Beats

Make this into a fun movement game by substituting gross-motor actions such as jumping, hopping, and stomping for the clapping.

WHAT TO DO:

1. Tell the children that words have beats. Ask, "Listen to these words. Can you hear that each of these words has one beat? *boy, girl, dog, cat, me, you.* Let's clap to each beat when we say each of those words again." Repeat the words, and clap as you say each one.

2. Say, "Listen to these words. Can you hear that these words have two beats? *children, mother, father, teacher.* Let's clap two times as we say each of those words again." Repeat the words, and clap as you say each syllable.

3. Say, "Let's find out how many beats there are in each of your names. When I say your name, let's clap one time for each beat." Go around and say each child's name, clapping on each syllable.

Letters

Learning names of letters and letter-sound matches are skills that often develop together. With continuing experience, children begin to correctly identify letters and match them with their sounds, particularly when the letters and sounds appear at the beginning of words.

Walk That Letter

This is a wonderful way to introduce letter recognition.

Preparation: Use masking tape to create a huge uppercase letter on the floor. Create a letter that is made by using continuous movement: *B, C, D, L, M, N, O, R, S, U, V, W,* and *Z.*

WHAT TO DO:

1. Tell the children that you will all try to walk the shape of a letter. Ask, "Who can walk on the letter *C* without stepping off onto the carpet?"

2. Let the children take turns trying to walk the shape of a *C* without stepping off. Note: If you are concerned that they will not wait patiently, consider creating more than one example of the letter.

3. Challenge them to move in other ways on and around the letter. Ask, "Who can move around the letter *C* without putting your feet on it?" "Who can jump on the shape of the *C*?" "Who can march on the shape of the *C*?" "Who can tiptoe on the shape of the *C*?"

4. Play the game again another day using a different letter.

What's That Letter?

The children find different ways to use their bodies while learning to recognize letters.

Preparation: You will need a marker and some construction paper for this activity. Write a large letter on a piece of paper.

WHAT TO DO:

1. Hold up a paper with a letter written on it. Ask, "What's the name of this letter?" Let the children tell you its name. "Mei Ling said it. It's the letter *M*."

2. Ask, "What sound does it make?" Encourage them all to make the /m/ sound.

3. Encourage the children to use a part of their bodies to show how that letter looks. Comment on their efforts: "Lisa is using her hands to make an *M*."

4. Encourage them to show how the letter looks by using a different part of their bodies. Comment on their choices.

5. Encourage them to use their whole bodies to make the letter shape.

See the Letter I See?

Encourage the children to recognize letters in various fonts, sizes, and settings.

WHAT TO DO:

1. Take the children on a walk in the neighborhood. Ask them to look for letters: "Do you see a letter written anywhere?" Talk about the letters they see.

2. Ask, "Can you make that letter in the air with your fingers, hands, or arms?" Encourage them to make the letter shape. Comment on their efforts.

3. Continue your walk. Say, "As we walk around the neighborhood, we'll see some letters. When you see a letter you'd like to show us, make it in the air with your fingers, hands, or arms. We'll all try to guess what it is. Each of us will have a turn."

Musical Letters

Discuss the concepts of *straight* and *curvy* with the children. Show them letters and discuss which ones have straight lines, curvy lines, or both.

Preparation: You will need index cards and a marker. Make several sets of cards, each with an uppercase letter on both the front and the back. Put the same letter on each side of a card so that, no matter how the card falls, the letter will be visible.

○ letters with curvy lines: *B, C, D, G, J, O, P, Q, R, S,* and *U*

○ letters with straight lines: *E, F, H, A, K, W, I, Z, L, M, N, T, V, X,* and *T*

○ letters with both curvy and straight lines: *B, D, G, J, P, Q,* and *R*

WHAT TO DO:

1. Scatter the cards around on the classroom floor.
2. Ask the children to jump around when you start the music. Tell them, "When the music stops, stand on a curvy letter."
3. Play some music and let them jump around. Stop the music, and encourage them to stand on a curvy letter. Comment on their choices: "What letter did you find, Stephen? Oh, you found a curvy *G*."
4. Ask the children to march around the room when you start the music. Tell them, "When the music stops, put your elbow on a letter with only straight lines."
5. Play some music and let them march around. Stop the music, and encourage them to stand on a straight letter. Comment on their choices: "Laura found a straight *T*."
6. Continue the game, this time asking them to creep around the room while the music is playing. Tell them to put their noses on a letter that has both straight and curvy lines when the music stops.

Mathematics 2

During the early childhood years, children are actively engaged in acquiring concepts related to organizing and classifying information. Those who have many hands-on experiences related to classification, patterning, measurement, and number concepts are more apt to feel comfortable thinking mathematically than those children who lack those opportunities.

Counting

While saying the names of numbers comes early to many preschoolers, recognizing numbers often takes longer.

How Many Do We Need?

Opportunities for counting various objects, movements, and settings occur throughout the day.

WHAT TO DO:

1. Incorporate counting into everyday tasks. For example, say, "We usually have twelve children in our class, but Joey is sick today. How many children are here today? Let's count."

2. Ask, "How many cups will we need for snack today? Let's count together."

3. Encourage the children to count a specific number of jumps: "Let's jump four times."

4. Encourage them to clap that many times, then to tap their toes that many times.

Let's Count the Steps

Make this activity more active by asking the children to jump, hop, or march instead of simply walking.

Preparation: You will need masking tape for this activity. Attach a 6' (or longer) piece of masking tape to the floor. For younger children, create an aisle with two parallel masking tape lines.

WHAT TO DO:

1. Ask a volunteer to walk on the tape (or between the two strips of tape) as you and the other children count his steps: "George, can you walk on the tape as we count?"

2. When the child reaches the other end of the tape, ask the children, "What number did we count to?" Let them tell you.

3. Ask another child to walk on the tape (or between the two strips of tape), this time taking bigger steps: "Gloria, can you walk on the tape with bigger steps and see how high we can count? With bigger steps it will be fewer numbers."

4. When the child reaches the other end, ask the children, "What number did we count to?" Let them tell you.

5. Ask a third child to walk on the tape (or between the two strips of tape), this time taking tiny steps: "Jack, walk on the tape with tiny steps, and we'll all count. If you walk on tiptoes will it take more or fewer numbers? We'll count."

6. When the child reaches the other end, ask the children, "What number did we count to?" Let them tell you.

How Many Are There?

By moving on various numbers of body parts, children improve their body awareness and motor planning.

WHAT TO DO:

1. Ask the children, "How many hands do you have?" Count with them.

2. Ask, "How many elbows do you have?" Count with them.

3. Ask, "Do you have some body parts that are pointy? How many?" Let the children tell you which body parts are pointy. Count those parts with them.

4. Ask the children to show how to move on two parts of their bodies. Encourage them to move in different ways, and comment on how they move.

5. Ask the children to try to move on three parts of their bodies. Encourage them to move in different ways, and comment on how they move.

6. Ask the children to move on two pointy parts of their bodies. Encourage them to move in different ways, and comment on how they move.

Let's Count the Letters in the Names

Most people feel special when they see their name in print.

Preparation: You will need index cards and a marker. Create a card with each child's name on it.

WHAT TO DO:

1. Show all the cards to the children. Ask, "Can you see Juan's name? How many letters are in his name? Let's count." Count with them.

2. Ask them to jump that many times: "*Juan* has four letters. Jump four times—one, two, three, four."

3. Ask, "Can you see Matilda's name? How many letters are in her name? Let's count." Count with them.

4. Ask the children to hop on one foot that many times.

5. Continue the activity, looking at each child's name. Count the letters and have the children do an action that many times, using a different movement for each name, such as the following:

    - ○ shake
    - ○ wiggle
    - ○ spin
    - ○ stand up and sit down
    - ○ clap
    - ○ tap your toes
    - ○ touch your knees
    - ○ blink

Numbers

Introducing young children to numbers prepares them for a lifetime of positive interactions with math. In contrast to counting, number recognition is the ability to visually recognize and name numbers.

What's My Number?

Giving each child her own number lends a sense of intrigue to this simple counting game.

Preparation: You will need index cards, enough for each child to have one, and a marker. Write one numeral 1–9 on each card.

WHAT TO DO:

1. Give each child a card with a number on it.

2. Ask a child to look at her card: "Rachel, can you hop the same number of times as the number on your card? Don't tell us what that number is. We'll count how many times you hop." Help if needed.

3. Count with the children as the first child hops. Ask, "Who can say the number that Rachel hopped?" Let the children answer.

4. Ask the child to show her card: "Now show us the number on your card, Rachel. You have a three. We counted three hops."

5. Continue the activity, letting each child have a turn jumping, hopping, or clapping the number of times as the number on her card. Everyone else will get a chance to count that number.

I Can Make a Number with My Friend

This partner game requires each child to visualize the number in order to make his body look that way.

Preparation: You will need nine index cards, each with a numeral 0–9 on it.

WHAT TO DO:

1. Show the children the cards with numbers from zero to nine. Identify each number.
2. Ask for two volunteers. Encourage them to use their bodies together to make the shape of a number. Tell them that the other children will guess what number they are making.
3. Invite the children to pair up and show a number using their bodies together. The other children will try to guess the numbers they are making.

I Can Feel That Number

In addition to having the children visualize each number, this activity enhances a child's sense of tactile processing.

WHAT TO DO:

1. Tell the children that each of them will write a number on the back of a friend using a finger. The friend will try to guess the number.
2. Ask for a volunteer. Using a finger, draw a number from zero to nine on the child's back. Ask, "Can you guess the number I'm writing on your back with my finger?" If she cannot guess, tell her the number.
3. Ask the children to pair up. Encourage them to write a number on their friends' backs with their fingers. Let the friends guess the numbers. When one of a pair guesses the number, they can switch and let the other person guess.

First, Second, Third, or Last?

Understanding ordinal numbers brings awareness of the placement of objects in a series.

WHAT TO DO:

1. Tell the children you are going to play a line-up game. Ask, "Joshua, would you please stand first in line?" Guide Joshua to the beginning of the line.

2. Ask a second child to join the first child: "Maria, would you be second in line, right behind Joshua?"

3. Continue, asking each child to join the line.

4. When all of the children are in line, ask, "Who's last in the line?"

5. Ask the children to sit down again.

6. This time, ask them to move into line in different ways. Say, "Let's make the line again, with Scott slithering to first place, Betty sliding to second place, and Dora jumping to third place." Give them time to move to the line.

7. Continue, saying, "Larry, hop on one foot to fourth place. Isaac, skip to fifth place. Sasha, move any way you like to last place." Give them time to join the line.

8. Ask the group to sit down, and continue with children who have not had a turn yet. Let each child have a chance to move to a place in line in his own special way.

One-to-One Correspondence

Based upon the idea that each object has the value of one, this is the process of touching one object for each number that is counted aloud. Children often touch or point to objects as they count, demonstrating their understanding of the number they have said.

Let's Play One-Two-Goose

This activity is a fun way to introduce the concept of one-to-one correspondence.

WHAT TO DO:

1. Have all of the students sit in a circle.
2. Explain that they will play a form of Duck-Duck-Goose, except that instead of saying *duck*, the person who is It

will count. He will say *goose* as he touches a child's head, and that child will chase him. If she catches the It person, he remains It. However, if the It person makes it around the circle and sits down in the empty spot, the new child becomes It.

3. Ask for a volunteer. Say, "Jack, can you go around the circle touching each child on the head as you count? Say, 'Goose!' to the one you'd like to have chase you." Let the volunteer practice counting as he touches each child's head. Help if necessary.

4. When the volunteer says, "Goose!" encourage the "goose" to chase the volunteer around the circle and touch him on the shoulder or back.

5. Continue the game, letting the children take turns being It and counting.

Count My Number

Adding movement to the activity allows the children to experience one-to-one correspondence in a new way.

Preparation: You will need index cards (enough for each child to have one) and a marker. Write a numeral 1–10 on each card.

WHAT TO DO:

1. Give a card to each child.

2. Ask, "What number is written on your card?" Let each child say the number she has.

3. Ask one child to do an action as many times as the number on his card: "Matan, you have a five. Can you bend over and touch your toes that many times? We'll all count with you." Encourage the children to count as he touches his toes.

4. Continue, inviting each child to demonstrate a movement as the class counts.

Help Set the Table for Snack

Children reinforce their knowledge of one-to-one correspondence as they participate in daily classroom routines.

WHAT TO DO:

1. Each day as you get ready for snack, ask a few children to be snack helpers. Part of a snack helper's job is to count the number of children and the items that the children will need. Ask a child to count the children and do a movement as he does so: "Nathan, how many children are here today? Please count them, touching each one as you jump from one child to the next." Help if needed.

2. When the first child has counted the children present, ask another snack helper to count the chairs: "Madison, how many chairs will we need for snack? How many children did Nathan count? Make sure there are that number of chairs at the snack table. As you count them, tiptoe from one chair to the next one and touch each one."

3. Ask other snack helpers to put out napkins, cups, and crackers for the children. Encourage them to move in different ways. Say, "Miriam, hop to the snack table and give everyone a napkin. Benjamin, bounce to the snack table and put a cup at each person's place. Tony, wiggle to the snack table and put a cracker at each person's place."

4. Tell the children that they will each get a turn to be a snack helper on other days.

How Many of Your Color Are There?

Children integrate their knowledge of one-to-one correspondence as they expand their awareness of the classroom environment.

Preparation: You will need construction paper in a variety of colors. Cut the paper into quarters to make color cards.

WHAT TO DO:

1. Give each child a color card.
2. Ask the children to walk around the room with their cards and count all the objects of that color out loud as they touch or point to them.
3. After the children have had time to walk around and find objects in their color, ask them to come back to the circle.
4. Invite a volunteer to talk about his color and the number of objects he found: "Brian, your card is blue. How many blue things did you find in this room? Can you show us the objects you found by counting them all out loud as you touch them with your elbow?"
5. Continue the activity, giving each child an opportunity to identify her color and to count the objects as she touches them with a body part, such as her chin, nose, or shoulder.

Shapes

Recognition of shapes is fundamental to understanding math. Beginning in infancy, children gain knowledge of shapes through many and varied visual and tactile experiences.

Can You Move on the Shape?

Inviting the children to pull up the masking tape at the end of this game adds a dimension of fine-motor and proprioceptive practice.

Preparation: You will need masking tape for this activity. Make a giant masking-tape shape, such as a circle, on the floor.

WHAT TO DO:

1. Encourage the children to walk on the shape by stepping on the tape. Let them take turns following the taped line. Comment as they move: "Jermaine, you are walking on the circle."

2. Challenge them to move in different ways as they follow the shape:
   ○ tiptoe
   ○ jump
   ○ slide sideways
   ○ walk backward

3. Vary the activity by making other shapes with the masking tape, such as a square, a rectangle, or a triangle.

What's That Shape?

Cleanup is a breeze as you ask the children to collect various shapes to bring back to you. Remember: Use this time to reinforce movement as well!

Preparation: Cut out a dozen of each of the following shapes from one color of paper: circles, squares, triangles, and rectangles. If the children are prepared for a greater challenge, use a variety of colors for the shapes.

WHAT TO DO:

1. Scatter the shapes all over the floor.
2. Hold up one of each of the shapes, and ask, "Who can tell me what this shape is?" Let the children identify each of the shapes.
3. Encourage the children to look around and find squares on the floor and stand on them.
4. Invite them to find circles and stand on them.
5. Continue, asking the children to find and stand on different shapes.
6. Tell the children that you will play some music. When the music stops, tell them that you will ask them to find a shape and touch it with the body part you name.
7. Play music, then stop it. Ask the children to put their noses on a triangle.
8. Continue with shapes and body parts such as follows:
   - Put one foot on a square and the other foot on a different shape.
   - Put one elbow on a circle.
   - Put one knee on a rectangle.
9. Add the dimension of color for older children: put your elbow on a red circle; put your foot on a blue triangle.

Let's Make Shapes

Figuring out how to move one's body to make a shape requires visualization and planning.

WHAT TO DO:

1. Discuss different shapes with the children. Show them examples of circles, squares, and triangles.

2. Ask the children to find a circle in the classroom and put an elbow on it.

3. Ask them to find a square and put a finger on it.

4. Ask them to find a triangle and put a foot on it.

5. Ask them to make their whole bodies look like a circle. Comment on their efforts: "Mattie is bending over to touch her toes to make a circle."

6. Continue, challenging the children to make shapes with their bodies. Comment on their efforts.

7. Encourage the children to make the shapes in other ways, such as the following:
   ○ with two fingers
   ○ with both arms
   ○ with one arm and one leg
   ○ with a friend

Making Stretchy Shapes

Elastic is a terrific tool for integrating proprioception into a variety of learning activities.

Preparation: You will need elastic tape, a needle, and thread. Cut one-yard lengths of the elastic tape, enough for each child to have one. Sew the two ends of each length together to create a loop.

WHAT TO DO:

1. Give each child a loop.
2. Ask, "How many sides does a triangle have?" Challenge the children to make their loops into triangles using three parts of their bodies.
3. Ask, "How many sides does a square have?" Challenge them to use four body parts to stretch their elastic into the shape of a square.
4. Ask, "How many friends do you need to make a standing-up triangle with one of the elastic tapes? Please show us." Let them experiment.
5. Ask, "How many friends do you need to make a standing-up square with one of the elastic tapes? Please show us."
6. Encourage them to make any shape they choose. Ask, "What shape are you making with your loop?"
7. Challenge the children to move around the room while maintaining their elastic shapes.

Colors

Learning about colors is an important milestone for children as they become more competent throughout their preschool years. Colors are all around us, making the lessons obvious and interesting for learners. Draw the children's attention to aspects in their environment by discussing colors, playing games focusing on colors, and naming colors.

Dancing with Your Ribbon

Using ribbons and music makes this activity a beautiful experience for the eyes and ears. When possible, make a video of it to share with the children.

Preparation: You will need colored ribbon in blue, green, yellow, and red. Cut the ribbon into lengths of approximately two feet.

WHAT TO DO:

1. Give each child a colored ribbon.
2. Play music and encourage the children to dance with their ribbons:
   - Ask, "Who has a blue ribbon? How can you dance to the music while waving your ribbon?"

- ○ Ask, "Who has a yellow ribbon? If you have a yellow ribbon, please join the children who are dancing with their blue ribbons."

3. Ask the children with yellow and blue ribbons to freeze. Ask, "Who has a green ribbon? Only those who have a green ribbon please dance to the music while waving your ribbons."

4. Continue the activity, naming different colors and asking different groups of children to dance with their ribbons and others to freeze. Say, "I'll keep saying different colors, and when I say your color you dance to the music with your ribbon. When I tell you to stop, just freeze where you are."

Let's Make a Color Bracelet

(Based on "Nature Bracelet" from *The Out-of-Sync Child Has Fun* by Carol Kranowitz.)

Children create a beautiful take-home reminder of the colors in nature.

Preparation: You will need masking tape for this activity.

WHAT TO DO:

1. Give each child a bracelet made of masking tape with the sticky side facing out.

2. Take the children on a nature walk. As you walk, ask them about the colors they see.

3. Ask, "Can you find some things that are green?" Encourage them to pick up something green and stick it to their bracelets. Note: Tell them not to stick a live insect or other creature to their bracelets. Leave the bugs where they are.

4. Continue, asking them to find the following:
   - ○ things that are red
   - ○ things that are brown

○ things that are blue

○ things that are yellow

Encourage them to pick the items up and stick them to their bracelets.

5. Talk with them about the different things they found.

Let's Play Traffic Light

Self-regulation is crucial in the classroom and in the world. The ability to stop, go, and move slowly translates readily into the ability to self-regulate.

Preparation: You will need paper plates, glue, and construction paper in red, yellow, and green. Cut one circle the size of a paper plate out of each color, and glue each onto a paper plate.

WHAT TO DO:

1. Tell the children you will play music, and they can dance. Tell them that when they see you hold up a green "light," they are to dance fast. When they see a yellow "light," they should dance slowly. When they see the red "light," they should stop.

2. Play music, and invite the children to dance as they wish.

3. Hold up the green light. Ask, "What can we do when we see this color?" Encourage them to show you.

4. Hold up the red light. Ask, "Can you show me what to do when you see this color?"

5. Hold up the yellow light. Ask, "Can you show what to do when you see this color?"

6. Continue encouraging the children to dance while occasionally holding up a color. Comment on their actions: "Stacey is dancing slowly. She sees me holding a yellow light."

Let's Play Tape Touch

In addition to learning colors and following directions, children practice fine-motor skills as they place and remove the tape.

Preparation: You will need masking tape or painter's tape in red, yellow, blue, and green.

WHAT TO DO:

1. Give each child a small piece of each of the tape colors.
2. Ask them to stick each piece of tape to the floor, anywhere they like. Then, ask them to smooth them out and rub them down hard with their hands. No piece should be on top of another piece of tape.
3. Say, "Put one hand on the red tape and one foot on the blue tape."
4. Continue, asking them to put different body parts on the different colors:
   - their heads on green tape
   - one elbow on blue tape and one knee on yellow tape
   - a round part of their bodies on red tape and a pointy part on blue tape

Patterns

A pattern is a sequence of repeating colors, sounds, or objects. The easiest patterns are those involving two variables, such as red, blue, red, blue, referred to as an ABAB pattern. More complex patterns include three elements, such as red, blue, green, red, blue, green, referred to as an ABC pattern. Identifying and creating patterns is the beginning of the mastery of lifelong mathematical skills. Help children recognize patterns through singing, movement, and many other classroom activities.

Can You Copy My Pattern?

Use simple patterns for younger children. Encourage more involved movements for those who are ready.

WHAT TO DO:

1. Encourage the children to copy you. Jump once and clap, and then repeat that sequence. Ask, "Can you do what I'm doing? I'm doing two things, one after the other, and then repeating that pattern. Let's keep making that pattern. Jump, clap, jump, clap."

2. Ask for a volunteer to make a different pattern. Say, "You make a pattern that we can all copy. Do two things with your body, repeat it, and we'll copy your pattern." Comment on the child's pattern: "Karen is doing a stomp-jump pattern. Let's copy her: stomp, jump, stomp, jump."

3. Continue, letting the children make up simple ABAB patterns for everyone to copy.

Making Patterns with Our Friends

This is a fun way to form a line when leaving the classroom.

WHAT TO DO:

1. Ask a child to jump to you: "Emilia, can you jump over here and stand next to me?"

2. Ask another child, "Sam, can you jump over and stand next to Emilia?"

3. Ask a third child, "Isabelle, can you jump to stand next to Sam?"

4. Ask a fourth child, "Mark, can you jump to stand next to Isabelle?"

5. Ask the class, "Who can tell us what this pattern is?" See if they can identify the girl, boy, girl, boy pattern.

6. Say, "Let's keep this pattern going. Who do we need next, a boy or a girl?" Encourage each child to jump to a place in line.

Copy My Sound

Using the auditory system lets children recognize that patterns are everywhere.

Preparation: You will need one pair of rhythm sticks for each child.

WHAT TO DO:

1. Give each child a set of rhythm sticks.

2. Tap out a pattern, such as ABAB or ABC. For example, hit the floor with both sticks and then hit them together.

3. Ask, "Who can copy my pattern?" Let the children copy you.

4. Tell them that you will do a different pattern. Hit the floor with one hand, then with the other hand, and then hit both sticks together (ABC).

5. Ask, "Who can copy this pattern? It's a little more difficult." Let the children copy you.

6. Ask each child in turn to create a pattern that the rest of you can copy.

Jumping Patterns

It is fun to play a game that incorporates colors, movement, patterns, and spatial awareness. Emphasize the safety aspect of being aware of one another.

Preparation: You will need red, blue, yellow, and green masking tapes.

WHAT TO DO:

1. Give each child a small piece of each of the colored masking tapes.

2. Let them put each piece on the floor in a separate place (no pieces on top of other pieces). Ask them to smooth the tape out and rub the pieces hard with their hands.

3. Challenge the children to jump on the tape in this pattern: red, red, blue. Say, "Everyone can jump around the room using this pattern. Be careful not to bump into your friends."

4. Ask each child in turn to create a pattern that everyone else can copy.

Sorting and Classifying

Sorting and classifying activities help children organize materials. Children can group objects together based on attributes such as color, shape, size, texture, flavor, or other characteristics. Draw their attention to items with different shapes, sizes, colors, and weights all around them.

How Many Brothers and Sisters Do You Have?

Introduce the concept of sorting and classifying by drawing on information that the children know best—themselves.

WHAT TO DO:

1. Ask the children to think about their families. Who are the members of their families?

2. Ask, "Do you have a brother? If so, jump five times." Encourage the children who have brothers to jump. Count with them as they do so.

3. Ask, "Do you have a sister? If so, twirl three times." Encourage the children who have sisters to twirl. Count with them as they do.

4. Ask, "Do you have no brothers or sisters? If so, bend over and touch your toes four times." Encourage the children who have no siblings to touch their toes. Count with them as they do.

5. Say, "If you have a brother and a sister, tap your shoulders six times." Encourage the children with both a brother and a sister to tap their shoulders. Count with them as they do.

Are You Alike or Different?

It is fun to copy your partner's movement. Creating a movement that is different from your partner's demonstrates a concrete understanding of the concept of *different*.

WHAT TO DO:

1. Ask the children to pair up.
2. Ask a pair to move in the same way: "Allison and Mark, can you two show us how each of you moves the same way as the other? Can you both spin in a circle?" As they spin, comment that they are moving alike. They are both spinning.

3. Ask them to move in two different ways: "Now can you show us how you move in different ways from each other? Allison, what will you do? Jump? And Mark, what will you do? Wiggle? Okay. Ready, go!" As they move, comment that they are moving differently. Allison is jumping, and Mark is wiggling.

4. Give each pair a chance to show how they can move the same way and in a different way from each other.

Let's Collect and Sort

Similarities and differences abound. Taking the children outside to select their own similar and different objects gives them an opportunity to move and to explore the world outside the classroom.

Preparation: You will need paper bags, one for each child.

WHAT TO DO:

1. Tell the children that you are going on a walk outside. While you walk, they will look for items to collect. Give each child a paper bag.

2. Tell the children to look for things to collect that are round, brown, or soft. Ask them to put those things in their bags.

3. After some time, ask, "Have you found things that are round, things that are brown, and things that feel soft?" Make sure each child has something for each category in his bag.

4. Return to the classroom, and ask the children to empty their bags, putting round things in a pile, brown things in another pile, and all the soft things in a third pile.

5. As they sort their items, talk with them about what they have found: "Herbie, you found a round rock." "Mary Beth, you found a brown stick." "Paul found a soft flower."

What Fits and What Doesn't?

Spatial awareness is fundamental to writing and mastering math concepts. While focusing on similarities and differences, children are developing their awareness of size and shape.

Preparation: You will need paper towel tubes cut in half, enough for each child to have one section. Provide an assortment of objects of various sizes.

WHAT TO DO:

1. Put the objects for sorting on a table. Give each child a tube section.

2. Help the children form groups of two or three, and give each group a pile of objects to sort.

3. Invite them to look through their piles and find the largest object. When they have found that object, ask them to put it through the opening of their tubes.

4. Continue encouraging the children to try all of their items. Ask them to make two piles: one with items that fit through the tube and the other with those that do not fit.

Science

When you provide active, varied, hands-on experiences that let children predict, observe, experiment, and conclude, you nurture a lifelong interest in investigative learning. While some scientific findings are obvious and concrete, others are less so, often seeming mysterious and even magical to young children. There are so many topics that can be the focus of early scientific investigations. We've chosen a few to present here—let these ideas inspire your own!

Comparing and Estimating

Children's understanding of attributes, such as size, weight, and volume, develops as they have hands-on experiences with touching, observing, comparing, and experimenting with objects.

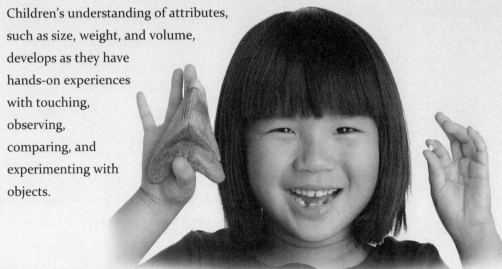

Are You Taller or Shorter?

Inviting the children to demonstrate concepts allows each child a chance to be active rather than just sitting and observing.

WHAT TO DO:

1. Ask two volunteers to stand back-to-back.
2. Ask the other children, "Who is taller, Vered or Michael?"
3. Ask, "Michael, how can you make your body as tall as Vered's?"
4. Ask, "Vered, how can you make your body shorter than Michael's?"
5. Ask all of the children to stand and pair up. Challenge them to make themselves taller than or shorter than their partners.

More or Fewer?

This is an engaging activity for rainy days as it allows the children to get out their wiggles.

WHAT TO DO:

1. Tell the children that you are going to talk about *more* and *fewer*. Begin by asking the boys to slither to one side of the room. Ask the girls to clomp to the other side of the room.
2. Ask, "Where are there more children, on the side with the girls or the side with the boys?" Count aloud the number in each group.
3. Say, "Everyone who is wearing blue, roll to the center of the room and sit there."
4. Together, count the blue and nonblue groups, and decide with the children which group has more and which group has fewer children.
5. Repeat the activity, varying the locomotor movements and the group descriptions.

Which Is Heavier, and Which Is Lighter?

Because proprioception—the awareness of sensations coming from muscles and joints—is crucial for handwriting, this is an outstanding prewriting activity.

Preparation: You will need a feather and a beanbag for each child.

WHAT TO DO:

1. Give each child a feather and a beanbag.
2. Ask the children to handle each item and compare their weights. Ask, "Which feels heavier, the feather or the beanbag? Which one feels lighter?"
3. Challenge them to predict which one would fall faster. Ask, "When I drop both the feather and the beanbag, which one do you think will touch the floor first?" Listen to their predictions.
4. Drop the beanbag and the feather at the same time. Ask, "Which one touched the floor first? Was it the one that was lighter or the one that was heavier?" Listen to their responses.
5. Encourage them to show how they can move lightly like the feather.
6. Encourage them to show how they can move heavily like the beanbag.

How Many Friends Will It Take?

This activity offers an opportunity for social development, spatial organization, and practice with counting and prediction.

WHAT TO DO:

1. Ask the children to stand and stretch out their arms to make a letter *T*.

2. Say, "Touch your fingertips to your friend's fingertips, keeping your arms stretched."

3. Ask them to predict how many friends it will take to stretch from one end of the classroom to the other, with their arms stretched out and fingertips touching.

4. Ask the children to stretch out their arms and touch a friend's fingertips, stretching in a line across the room.

5. Count with them how many friends it takes to span the room. Ask, "Was your prediction more or fewer children than it actually took?"

6. Challenge them to stretch across the room in other ways:
    - ❍ hands down and elbows touching
    - ❍ arms at their sides and shoulders touching
    - ❍ lying down in a straight line with everyone facing the same way (one person's head touching another person's feet)
    - ❍ lying down side-to-side with shoulders touching

    Each time, ask them to predict the number it will take to span the room, and count with them how many friends it actually takes.

Spatial Relationships

Spatial relationships are associations between two or more objects and include concepts such as position, distance, and direction. Using prepositions, such as *toward*, *through*, *under*, *over*, *to*, *at*, *by*, *on*, *in*, and *out*, throughout the day can help the children understand and be aware of spatial relationships.

Can You Go Over, Under, Around, and Through?

Obstacle courses are wonderful tools for helping children understand spatial relationships and can be made from almost anything. They can be constructed in a circle or as transitional tools to help move the children from place to place.

Preparation: You will need a variety of obstacles, such as large boxes or tunnels to creep through, tables to crawl under, mats to climb over, and boxes to walk around.

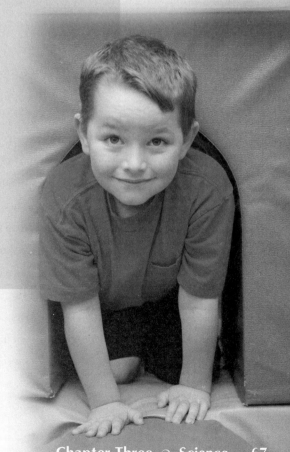

WHAT TO DO:

1. Create an obstacle course. Vary the levels of obstacles so that the course will feature the following:
   - ○ moving over is followed by moving under
   - ○ moving around is followed by moving through
   - ○ moving through is followed by moving over

   Try to avoid bottlenecks, and make sure that you can see the children as they move through the course.

2. Let the children take turns as they explore the course. Comment as they explore: "Karl, you are creeping through the tunnel." "Abbey, you are crawling under the table."

Dancing with a Partner

Integrating body awareness and music makes this partner activity challenging and fun. It can be easily modified for various developmental abilities.

Preparation: Plastic hoops, one for every two children.

WHAT TO DO:

1. Invite the children to choose partners. Give one hoop to each pair of children, and play some music.

2. Ask the pairs to move to the music while they are both inside the hoop. Let them dance.

3. Ask the pairs to move to the music while they are both outside the hoop. Let them dance.

4. Ask the pairs to dance to the music with one of them inside and the other outside the hoop.

5. Ask them to dance with the hoops in a variety of ways:
   - ○ one foot inside the hoop and the other foot outside the hoop
   - ○ one hand inside the hoop and the other hand outside the hoop
   - ○ their bottoms inside and their feet outside the hoop

Can You See Me?

This version of Hide and Seek is delightful to watch in action and is an opportunity for taking wonderful photos.

Preparation: You will need large boxes (big enough for a child to crawl inside). Provide a box for each pair of children.

WHAT TO DO:

1. Invite the children to pair up. Give each pair a large box.
2. Ask the children to take turns getting inside their boxes so that no part of them is showing.
3. Ask them to take turns putting their heads and one foot outside the box while everything else stays inside the box.
4. Ask them to use the boxes in a variety of ways:
   - one hand and one foot outside the box
   - one shoulder outside the box
   - two feet and one hand outside the box
   - their head in the box and everything else outside the box

Pass the Ball

Crossing the midline—the ability to cross the vertical center of the body—is fundamental for writing. Midline crossing develops anytime between four and six years of age. Using both hands requires children to cross the midline as they pass the ball.

Preparation: You will need a ball or a beanbag. Older children can use a ball, and younger ones can use a beanbag.

WHAT TO DO:

1. Ask the children to stand in a circle while facing in the same direction, back to front.

2. Ask the children to pass the ball sideways with two hands to the person behind them. Say, "Let's pass the ball all around the circle back to the beginning."

3. Ask the children to pass the ball sideways with two hands to the person in front of them.

4. Ask the children to pass the ball over their heads to the person behind them.

5. Ask the children to pass the ball between their legs to the person behind them.

6. For an extra challenge, older children can alternate passing the ball over and under to those behind them.

Water

Water play should always be available. It offers a multitude of open-ended learning opportunities for preschoolers. As children manipulate objects in water, they observe why and how things happen, try new ideas, and explore possible solutions.

Beat the Water

This is a fun exploration to do outdoors on a warm day. Be sure to have towels on hand.

Preparation: You will need eggbeaters, dish detergent, and water in a water table or tub.

WHAT TO DO:

1. Show the children an eggbeater. Ask them if they know what it is. Listen to their responses.
2. Encourage the children to predict what will happen when you beat the water with the eggbeaters. Listen to their ideas.
3. Beat the water with the eggbeaters. Were the children's predictions correct?
4. Ask, "What will happen if I add a few drops of liquid dish detergent to the water and you beat it?" Listen to their predictions.
5. Add a few drops of detergent to the water, and let the children explore what happens when they use the eggbeaters in the soapy water.
6. When they have had turns playing in the water, ask them to show you with their bodies how the water looks before it is beaten with the eggbeaters.
7. Ask, "Can you show me with your bodies how the water looks while it is being beaten with the eggbeaters?"

What Happened to the Water?

Take the children outside on a bright, sunny day, and find a cement sidewalk for them to paint. Encourage them to use big, long movements and to predict as they observe the results of their efforts.

Preparation: You will need paintbrushes and buckets of water.

WHAT TO DO:

1. Give each child a paintbrush. Set out the buckets of water for them to use.

2. Ask the children to show you how to paint the sidewalk with water. Encourage them to use big, long strokes and to cover the whole sidewalk, making it completely wet.

3. When they have explored painting with water, take a break for snack. Ask, "What do you think the sidewalk will look like when we come back here after snack?" Let the children make predictions. Say, "We'll come back then and see if you're right."

4. After snack, bring them back outside and observe the sidewalk. Ask, "What has happened? Where has the water gone?" Talk with them about evaporation.

5. Let them continue to explore painting with water.

What Freezes, and What Melts?

The warmer the weather, the quicker the result, and the more comfortable the children will feel working with the ice.

Preparation: You will need plastic bowls and ice cubes.

WHAT TO DO:

1. Give the children plastic bowls filled with ice cubes, and let them play outside, exploring on their own.

2. As they play, ask them for ideas for things to do with ice cubes. Suggest a few ideas such as the following:
   ○ Can you stir with them?
   ○ What if you stack them on top of each other?
   ○ Can you pour them out of the bowl?
   ○ Can you build with them?
   ○ Can you paint with them?

   Encourage them to try doing each of those things with the ice cubes and see what happens.

3. Ask, "Can you show me with your body how an ice cube looks right when you take it out of the freezer?" "Can you show me with your body what the ice cube looks like when it starts to melt?" "Show me with your body what it looks like when it's all melted."

4. Before you head inside for another activity, say, "Let's put the ice cubes in the bowl and come back later to see if they look different from the way they look now. Show me with your body what you think they will look like."

Watch the Drops of Water

Excellent for exercising fine-motor and eye-hand coordination, this activity can be played indoors or out.

Preparation: You will need one medicine dropper per child and small paper cups, enough for each child to have two. For each pair of cups, put water in one and leave the other one empty.

WHAT TO DO:

1. Give each child a medicine dropper and two cups, one containing water and the other empty.
2. If the children are not familiar with how to use a medicine dropper, show them how to use it.
3. Ask, "How can you use your dropper to put some water into the empty cup?"
4. Encourage the children to predict how many drops it will take to cover the bottom of their cups. Listen to their guesses.
5. Let them experiment and see how many drops of water it takes to cover the cup bottom.

Shadows

The outdoors is a terrific natural laboratory for exploring light and shadows. Adults can nurture children's interest by commenting on shadows and suggesting opportunities for further exploration. Experiments can move inside the classroom, too, with the use of flashlights and lamps.

Did You See the Shadows on the Nature Walk?

Shadows are all around us, but only when the sun is out. Take advantage of a beautiful day, and explore shadows with the children.

WHAT TO DO:

1. Take the children on a walk in the neighborhood on a sunny day. Ask them to look for shadows that are made by trees, bushes, cars, and houses.

2. Ask, "Can you jump on a shadow made by a tree?" Let them find shadows to jump on.

3. Ask, "Can you stand on one foot on a shadow made by a bush?" "Can you tiptoe around a shadow made by a flagpole?"

4. Encourage them to interact any way they like with the shadows they see around them.

Watch My Shadow Grow

Though best played outdoors, this activity can be moved indoors with the use of a bright lamp or flashlight.

WHAT TO DO:

1. Take the children outside to a sunny area. Ask, "Can you see your shadow?" Let the children look around for their shadows and their friends' shadows.

2. Ask, "What happens to your shadow when you stretch your arms over your head?" Encourage them to stretch really high and pay attention to what happens.

3. Ask the children to experiment with their shadows in other ways, such as the following:

   ○ standing while balancing on one foot

   ○ stretching arms out to the sides

   ○ bending over and touching toes

4. Say, "Let's make our shadows":

○ taller	○ thinner
○ shorter	○ straight
○ wider	○ curved

5. Encourage the children to suggest other ways to change their shadows.

Let's See a Shadow-Puppet Show

Copying a shadow's movements presents a far greater challenge than copying a person's movements. Children younger than four may find this activity too difficult.

Preparation: You will need a bedsheet or large piece of light-colored fabric and a flashlight or bright lamp. Hang the sheet vertically from a high place. Place the light behind the sheet.

WHAT TO DO:

1. Ask a child to stand behind the sheet. Encourage him to move his body in a silly way.

2. Ask, "Can you children who are in front of the sheet tell us what you see?"

3. Tell the child behind the sheet that you and the other children will watch his shadow move and will copy what he does.

4. Invite each of the children to take a turn making shadows for the others to copy.

Trace My Shadow

In addition to a sunny day, you will need a rather large concrete space for this activity.

Preparation: You will need enough sidewalk chalk for each child to have a piece.

WHAT TO DO:

1. Take the children outside to a sidewalk that is in the sun for most of the day.

2. Ask them to find their shadows on the sidewalk.

3. Ask the children to select partners, and give each pair a piece of chalk.

4. Ask one child of each pair to stand very still in an unusual position, such as on one foot or with one hand on a hip.

5. Invite the other child to trace around her partner's shadow.

6. Let each child of the pair have a turn tracing.

7. Ask the children to look at all the drawings their class has made. Challenge them to find the outlines of their own shadows.

Magnets

As children interact with magnets, they note that some objects are attracted by magnetic force while others are not. They also learn that, while they cannot see magnetic force, it is possible to observe what it does.

What Can We Do with Magnets?

The mystery of magnets is often exciting to children. Using their bodies to reinforce the concept is an intriguing way to work on proprioception and motor planning.

Preparation: You will need enough magnets for each child to have one and a variety of metallic and nonmetallic objects.

WHAT TO DO:

1. Provide the children with magnets, some metallic objects, and some nonmetallic objects.
2. Encourage the children to explore ways to use the magnets, touching them to different objects and surfaces and observing what "sticks." Note: Let them know that certain objects, such as computers and cell phones, should not be touched with magnets.
3. After they have had some time to explore the magnets, ask, "What did you do with your magnets?" Let them tell you how they explored the way magnets work.
4. Encourage the children to talk about which items and surfaces stuck to their magnets and which did not.
5. Expand their understanding by asking, "Can you pretend that your feet are magnets?" and "Can you predict what will happen when you move around the room with all of your magnetic-footed friends?"

6. Now ask them to pretend that the floor is a magnet. Ask, "If your feet were made of wood, how could you move around?" "If your feet were made of metal, what would happen? Show us."

7. Encourage them to pretend that different body parts are magnets:
   - ○ elbows
   - ○ knees
   - ○ head

How Many Paper-Clip Friends Are There?

This game requires a rather large space as the children pretend to be magnets and paper clips. Inviting them to move in novel ways adds an additional dimension to the game.

Preparation: You will need magnets, metal paper clips, and a large space.

WHAT TO DO:

1. Demonstrate to the children how a magnet can attract a paper clip. Then, demonstrate how that paper clip becomes a magnet to attract another paper clip. Investigate how many paper clips can be attracted in the chain.

2. Let the children experiment with the magnets and paper clips.

3. Gather the children, and tell them that they will pretend to be magnets and paper clips. Say, "Let's pretend Victor is a magnet. Everyone else is a paper clip. Victor will move around the room and grab a paper-clip friend by the hand. That friend will grab another paper-clip friend. We will continue until we have all of the friends in a chain."

4. Let the children pretend to be paper clips attracted to the magnet. After a while, let another child be the magnet.

Safety Note: Please refer to the safety disclaimer on page 2.

Can Magnets Pull through Objects?

Because this activity requires children to have a well-developed sense of laterality—the ability to move one hand independently of the other—it should not be introduced to children younger than four. If the children find it too difficult to hold the plate while moving their magnet hands, they can partner with a friend. One child can hold the plate while the other child moves the magnet.

Preparation: You will need a paper plate, a magnet, and a paper clip for each child. Provide objects to test with the magnets, such as plastic lids, cardboard pieces, screws, and rubber bands.

WHAT TO DO:

1. Place a paper clip on top of a paper plate and a magnet under the plate. Show the children how the magnet will move the paper clip around.

2. Give each child a paper plate, a magnet, and a paper clip, and let them explore moving the paper clip with the magnet.

3. Ask, "Can you move the paper clip with other materials between it and the magnet, such as a table, a chair seat, or a piece of fabric? What do you notice? Does the magnet work better with some materials than with others?"

4. Give the children objects to place on top of the plate, such as plastic lids, cardboard pieces, screws, and rubber bands.

5. Ask, "Can you move the magnet below the plate and see if the object on top moves? What things moved? What things didn't move?"

6. Ask the children to think about and explain why the magnet works with some materials but not with others. Listen to their responses—they may be quite creative!

7. Say, "Choose a partner. Pretend that one of you is a magnet and the other one is a paper clip. When the magnet moves, the paper clip moves with it. Now, move around the room. I'll let you know when it's time to switch places with your partner."

Let's Go Fishing

You can adapt this delightful eye-hand coordination game by suggesting that the children draw pictures of items to be fished. Attach washers, bolts, or coins to the backs of the "fish." Varying the weights of the metal pieces adds a proprioceptive aspect as well.

Preparation: Make pretend fishing rods by tying 12" lengths of string to sticks and then tying a magnet to the other end of each string. Make one for each child.

You will also need a basin or tub of water and a variety of items to put in the basin: erasers, paper clips, child-safe scissors, screws, nuts, bolts, rubber bands, cork, plastic lids, plastic blocks, wooden pencils, and wooden blocks.

WHAT TO DO:

1. Give a fishing rod to each child. Set out the basin of water, and put the variety of items in the water.
2. Encourage the children to predict what they might catch with their fishing rods: "Larry, when you go fishing in the water, what do you think will stick to the magnet on your fishing rod?"
3. Let them try to catch items with their fishing rods. As they play, ask them what is sticking to the magnet and what is not.
4. Ask them to fish for specific items:
   ○ one nut and one screw
   ○ one screw and one bolt
   ○ two paper clips

Magnification

A fascinating new world opens up to children as they explore with magnifiers, examining objects closely and noticing details not visible to the naked eye. Encourage them to explore, investigate, manipulate, and examine items both inside and outside the classroom.

What Does the Magnifying Glass Tell Us?

The children have opportunities to play detective as they use magnifying glasses to explore their world.

Preparation: You will need a magnifying glass for each child.

WHAT TO DO:

1. Give each child a magnifying glass, and ask them to look through the glasses at the items around them, such as the carpet, their hands, and their shoes.
2. Ask, "What does the magnifying glass help you see? Do things look different when you look through it?" Let them describe what they notice when they look through the magnifying glasses.
3. Ask, "Do things look bigger or smaller when you look through the magnifying glass?"
4. Say, "The word *magnify* means 'to make things look bigger.' I am going to come around with my pretend magnifying glass, and when I look through it, your body will

look much bigger. How can you make the body part I'm looking at be very, very big?"

○ Stand back and look at their whole bodies: "Make your whole bodies look magnified, as big as you can!"

○ Look at their hands: "Make your hands look magnified."

○ Look at their mouths: "Make your mouth look bigger."

○ Look at their arms: "Make your arms as big you can."

As they make themselves look bigger, comment on what they are doing: "Joye is stretching really big!"

Stretchy Pictures

To comfortably hold a pencil, children need good tactile processing. Good proprioception ensures that they know how hard to push in order to write. This activity is a fun way to develop both tactile and proprioceptive processing.

Preparation: Combine two parts white glue with one part concentrated liquid starch, which is usually found in supermarket laundry sections. Add food coloring, if desired. Stir, then let the mixture sit for five minutes. Knead the dough for about ten minutes to a smooth consistency. Divide it into pieces, one for each child.

You will also need some newspaper, preferably colorful, child-appropriate comics.

WHAT TO DO:

1. Give each child a ball of stretchy dough. Encourage them to stretch it and play with it. Let them try to bounce it.

2. Give the children some colorful Sunday comics from the newspaper. Ask them to put their stretchy dough on a picture and press it flat as hard as they can.

3. Ask them to gently peel the stretchy dough away from the picture. Say, "Look at the stretchy dough. What do you see?" They should see the picture on the stretchy dough.

4. Ask, "Can you gently stretch your dough pictures to magnify them?"

5. Ask, "Can you compare your stretchy dough pictures to the ones on the newspaper? Which one is the magnified one?"

Let's Magnify Our Sounds

Seeing the results of magnification is different from hearing the results. Growing their sounds from tiny and little to big and loud, children discover another way of understanding magnification.

WHAT TO DO:

1. Ask the children to make tiny little sounds on the floor with their hands. Comment on their efforts: "Mickey is making tiny little sounds with her fingertips."

2. Ask them how they can magnify the sound so that it is really big. Let them make great big sounds on the floor with their hands.

3. Encourage them to make tiny little sounds using different parts of their bodies:
    ○   with their feet on the floor
    ○   using one foot on the floor
    ○   with their elbows

4. Encourage them to make great big magnified sounds using the same parts of their bodies.

Let's Find Our Names

Working with magnifying glasses, children find the letters in their names. They can glue the letters onto craft sticks to create bookmarks. Adding a pin to the back makes a charming piece of personalized jewelry.

Preparation: You will need alphabet noodles, magnifying glasses, and dark construction paper, enough for each child.

WHAT TO DO:

1. Give each child a piece of dark construction paper. Sprinkle a small quantity of alphabet noodles onto the paper.
2. Encourage the children to use their magnifying glasses to find the first letter of their names. When they find the letter, suggest that they move it to the side.
3. Invite them to continue in the same manner, using the magnifying glass to look for each letter in their names.
4. Help them as needed, and comment as they search: "Brittany has found a *B*, an *R*, and an *I*. Now she's looking for a *T*."
5. For added fun, add alphabet noodles to soup for a yummy snack. Suggest that the children look for the letters of their names at snack time.

Social Studies

Children formulate many of their values and attitudes toward society in the early years. While there are many possibilities for social studies curriculum activities, the choice of specific activities to include in the classroom depends upon the children's interests and developmental levels. This curriculum area informs children as they investigate classroom, neighborhood, and community issues, exposing them to a broad variety of opinions.

About Me

This is a wonderful topic for building self-esteem, helping the children get to know each other, and developing class unity. Children learn best when they feel good about themselves, contributing to a positive attitude and bolstering their self-confidence.

How Do I Sound and Look?

A wonderful way to introduce the children in the class, this activity can also be fun after vacations when the children have not seen each other for a while.

WHAT TO DO:

1. Encourage the children to think of a unique way to move. Tell them that they will have a chance to show their friends their special ways of moving.

2. Ask for a volunteer to show her movement. Ask, "Sydney, can you introduce yourself by saying your name and making a special movement?" Encourage the children to watch her movement carefully.

3. Ask the children so say hi to Sydney while copying her movement: "Hi, Sydney! Sydney turned around in a circle. Let's turn in a circle, too."

4. Continue, letting each child have a chance to say his name and make a special movement, as the other children respond.

This Is My Family

Besides working on awareness of space, this activity is quite a good listening game.

WHAT TO DO:

1. Divide the class into two groups, and ask each group to stand on opposite sides of the room facing each other.

2. Tell the children that you will ask different questions about families. When they hear a question that reminds them of their own family, they can move to the other side of the room.

3. Ask, "Who has a brother? If you do, jump on two feet to the other side of the room. Be very careful not to bump into your friends." Let the children who have a brother jump across the room.

4. Ask, "Who has a sister? If you do, slide on your tummy to the other side of the room."

5. Continue, asking questions about families such as the following:

    ○   If you have a pet dog, hop across the room.

    ○   If you have a fish, twirl across the room.

    ○   If you have five people in your family, walk in a zigzag pattern across the room.

    ○   If you're the oldest child in your family, wave your arms in the air as you walk across the room.

    ○   If you're the youngest child in your family, wiggle your hips as you walk across the room.

    ○   If you have a grandparent who lives with you, move like an airplane across the room.

    ○   If there's something special about you, clap your hands as you walk across the room.

Flat Me

While this activity involves teacher preparation before it is introduced to the children, it is very well worth the time spent. Children make their own Flat Me, which can be used throughout the year to develop body awareness, spatial awareness, and motor planning.

Preparation: Provide life-sized paper shapes of the following body parts:

- head
- torso
- upper arms
- lower arms

- hands
- feet
- upper legs
- lower legs

You will also need brads, scissors, hole punches, markers, and crayons. Cut out enough parts for each child to assemble a complete paper body.

WHAT TO DO:

1. Ask the children to look at their real bodies. How many feet do they have? How many legs? How many arms? How many heads? Tell them that they will make Flat Mes out of paper to look like their real bodies.

2. Give each child the body parts she needs to make a Flat Me. Give them hole punches. Show them how to punch a hole in the paper. Give them brads, and show them how they work.

3. Help attach brads in the joints designated as the neck, shoulders, elbows, knees, hips, hands, and ankles, attaching all of the body parts appropriately. Ask: "Where does your paper head go on this paper body? Let's punch holes in the paper head and paper neck and then connect the head to the neck with the brads." Help them as needed.

4. Ask, "Now, can you touch your shoulder? What's attached to your shoulder? The places where our bodies bend are called *joints*. Connect the upper arms to the shoulders of your Flat Me."

5. Continue, helping the children to connect the following body parts:
    ○ lower and upper arms at the elbows
    ○ hands and lower arms at the wrists
    ○ upper legs and torso at the hips
    ○ upper and lower legs at the knees
    ○ feet and lower legs at the ankles

6. When they have assembled their Flat Mes, encourage them to use crayons and markers to decorate their cutouts as they wish.

7. When the children are finished, ask them to place their Flat Mes on the floor in different positions by moving the body parts.

Can You See My Flat Me?

Invite older children to copy their Flat Mes' positions by drawing the positions onto paper. Take photographs of the children in various positions. Invite them to make their Flat Mes look like the child in the photograph.

WHAT TO DO:

1. Using the Flat Mes the children have made, ask them to position their cutouts on the floor. Ask, "Johnny, can you place your Flat Me on the floor in any position you'd like?" When he has positioned his cutout, ask Johnny to position his real body to imitate the Flat Me.

2. Ask the other children to make their real bodies look like Johnny's Flat Me.

3. Ask, "Suzie, can you place your Flat Me on the floor in a position different from Johnny's?" Ask the other children to make their bodies look like Suzie's Flat Me.
4. Give each child an opportunity to position his Flat Me, imitate it, and let the other children imitate it as well.

About My Places

Children learn best when they feel that their world is safe and comfortable. Helping them learn about the environment in which they spend much of their waking time facilitates those feelings. Making maps can help them feel physically connected to their places.

This Is My Classroom

This is a great activity to do at the beginning of the year as well as anytime you wish to introduce a new center.

WHAT TO DO:
1. Lead the children on a walk around the classroom, pointing out centers and discussing activities to do there.
2. When you are finished with your tour, ask the children, "Who would like to go to the dress-up center? If so, please hop there."
3. Ask, "Who would like to cook dinner for your family? If so, please walk sideways to the center where you can do that."
4. Continue, inviting the children to perform a movement to get them to the centers where they want to play.

This Is My House

Using scissors and glue is a developmentally appropriate prewriting activity. The houses created in this activity can be used later as props in spatial and directional games.

Preparation: You will need old magazines, child-safe scissors, glue, and an empty cardboard box for each child.

WHAT TO DO:

1. Ask the children to think about their homes. What do they sit on? What do they sleep on? Where are their meals prepared? Where do they take a bath or brush their teeth? Talk with them about the features of their homes.

2. Provide an assortment of magazines, scissors, and glue. Give each child a box.

3. Ask the children to find pictures in the magazines of things they have in their homes, such as chairs, tables, beds, refrigerators, and windows.

4. Ask them to cut out those pictures and paste them onto their boxes.

5. When they are finished, invite each child to talk about his box.

This Is My Neighborhood

Introducing the challenge of using various body parts to glue the pictures adds a dimension of proprioceptive awareness to this arts-and-crafts activity.

Preparation: You will need a large piece of butcher or bulletin board paper, child-safe scissors, old magazines, and paste or glue. On the large sheet of paper, sketch a representation of your school building.

WHAT TO DO:

1. Walk through the neighborhood of the school with the children, pointing out hills, trees, buildings, people, vehicles, roads, and animals.

2. Upon returning to the classroom, place a large sheet of paper with a representation of the school building on the classroom floor. Provide an assortment of magazines, scissors, and paste or glue for each child.

3. Talk with the children about what you saw on your walk. Help them recall the hills, trees, streets, buildings, and cars.

4. Ask them to look in the magazines for pictures of some of the things you saw on your walk. Encourage them to cut out the pictures.

5. When each child has several picture cutouts, encourage them to paste or glue their pictures on the paper. Ask them to make sure their pictures stick to the paper by rubbing them with different body parts:
   - ○ hand
   - ○ knee
   - ○ elbow

This Is My School

Challenging children to map their environment teaches spatial awareness and directionality, both of which are underlying skills for neat and organized written work.

Preparation: You will need a large piece of butcher or bulletin board paper and some markers or crayons.

WHAT TO DO:

1. Lead the children through the school building, stopping at the front office, the administrator's office, the library, and any other place that the children may know about. Introduce the children to the important people who work in the school building.

2. When you return to the classroom, clear a space on the floor and spread out a huge sheet of paper.

3. Work with the children to draw a map of the building on the paper. Ask, "Where should we draw the front door on this map of our building?" Let the children tell you, and either draw the front door or ask a volunteer to draw it.

4. Ask, "If the front door is here, where should we draw our classroom?" Let the children show you where the classroom belongs, and either draw it or invite a volunteer to do so.

5. Ask the children to name other places in the building. Ask them to show you where on the map the places belong.

6. "Walk" through the finished map with the children, retracing with your finger the route that you took on your tour.

7. Tell the children that you will leave the big map on the floor, and during activity time they can practice remembering where things are by using their fingers to show where the class walked today.

About the World in Which We Live

As children's awareness expands beyond self-interest to the people and places around them, they become increasingly curious and better prepared to meet new experiences.

We Learn from Special Visitors

Discussing community helpers and their work provides ample opportunities for perceptual motor experimentation.

WHAT TO DO:

1. Invite different members of the community to visit the class and share information about their jobs. For instance, consider inviting firefighters, members of the police force, librarians, cashiers, waitresses, garbage collectors, barbers, clergy, and medical professionals.

2. Following a community member's visit, ask the children, "What did you learn from our special visitor today?"

3. Listen as they describe the tools and equipment that community member uses.

4. Depending on the job the visitor does, ask the children to move like the community member or like the tools he uses, such as the following:
   - barber's scissors: hold arms apart overhead and stand with legs apart to show open scissors; hold arms together straight above the head and stand with legs together to show closed scissors
   - garbage collectors: pretend to lift heavy trash cans up and over as they dump trash into their trucks

○ firefighters: pretend to climb ladders up, up, up and down, down, down

○ police: pretend to direct traffic by pointing in different directions

Let's Be a Book at the Library

Introduce this useful activity before or after a trip to the library.

WHAT TO DO:

1. Ask, "Who has been to a library? What did you do there?" Listen as the children tell about their experiences in the library and the things one finds and does there.

2. Ask, "How do we hold a book when we're reading it?" Let the children pretend to hold a book.

3. Say, "Books open and close. Open and close your hands the way you'd open and close a book." Let the children pretend to open and close a book.

4. Encourage them to stand up and open and close their legs as if they are books. Challenge them to lie down and open and close their legs as if they are books.

5. Show a real book, opening and closing it and turning the pages carefully, while emphasizing the importance of taking good care of it.

6. Say, "Pretend your body is a book. Show me the way your pages turn."

Let's Plant a Garden

Lessons learned at this age about taking care of the earth can affect children's attitudes toward environmental issues later. Everyone can participate in creating a garden, caring for plants, and enjoying the benefits of beautiful growing flowers and vegetables. Digging, pulling, carrying, and pouring are excellent prewriting activities.

WHAT TO DO:

1. Ask, "Has anyone here ever planted a garden? Let the children talk about their experiences. If you have a class garden, talk about what you do when you work in it.

2. Ask, "What do we need to plant a garden?" Let them tell you the items you need, such as shovels for digging, seeds for planting, watering cans or a hose, and baskets for collecting.

3. Invite the children to pretend to plant a garden. Ask them to show you how to use a pretend shovel to dig in your garden.

4. Continue pretending to plant your garden. Water the plants, pull the weeds, pick the ripe vegetables, and put them in a basket.

5. Take the children outside to work in your real garden.

Let's Make Snacks from Other Places

Introduce the children to foods from around the world. Prepare and taste examples of international foods, such as fried rice from China, moon cookies from Vietnam, deviled eggs from Germany, edamame from Japan, pizza from Italy, hummus and pita chips from the Middle East, and guacamole and chips from Mexico. Fine-motor movements required in preparing these foods will aid in prewriting skills.

Preparation: You will need a globe or a world map. Choose a new food to prepare with the children, and provide the ingredients. For this example, we will prepare guacamole. Chop some tomatoes and onion (if desired) ahead of time.

WHAT TO DO:

1. Show the children a map of the world. Ask, "Have you ever tasted guacamole? It comes from a country called Mexico. Here it is on the map." Show the children where your country is and where Mexico is.

2. Ask the children to help you make some guacamole. Show them the avocadoes, tomatoes, fresh cilantro, onion (if desired), and lime. Let them smell the ingredients. Say, "Here are all the items we need to make today's snack. We'll need to chop, mash, and stir, and everyone will have something to do."

3. Let the children help by washing the ingredients, scooping the pulp from the avocadoes, mashing the avocado, tearing the cilantro, squeezing the lime juice, adding the tomato and onion, and stirring everything together.

4. Let the children set out plates and napkins, put out chips for everyone, and scoop some guacamole on each plate.

5. Encourage them to try the yummy snack.

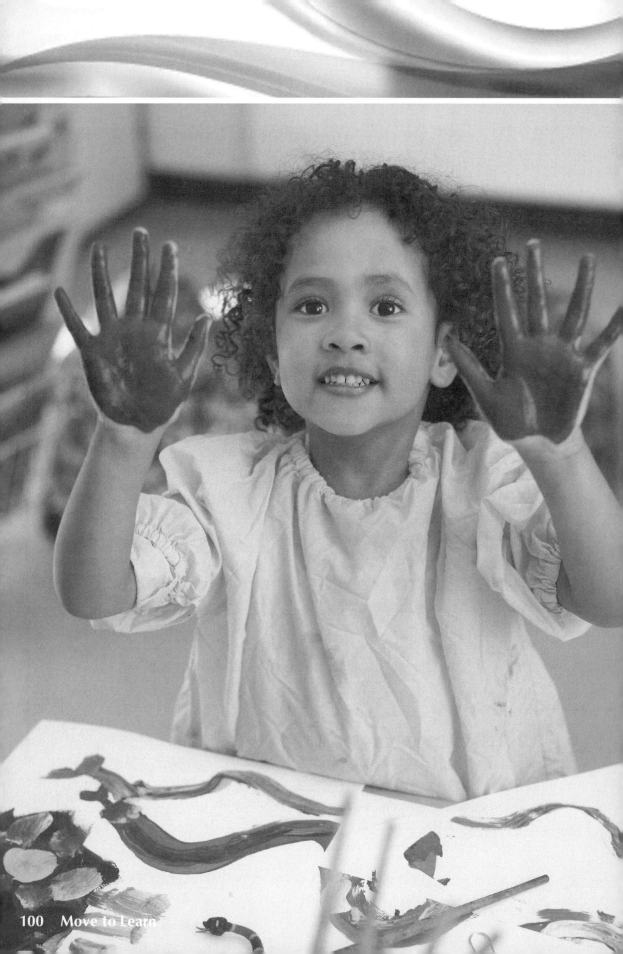

Creative Representation

Painting

Painting offers a way for children to develop their motor skills, an appreciation for others' works, and appreciation of their own creativity. It is a way for them to investigate colors, textures, and shapes while exploring process and outcome. As children paint, they convey ideas verbally and nonverbally, and we gain insight into the way they perceive their world, contributing to our understanding of their developmental abilities and interests. Painting, a great source of sensory stimulation, can be done with a variety of instruments.

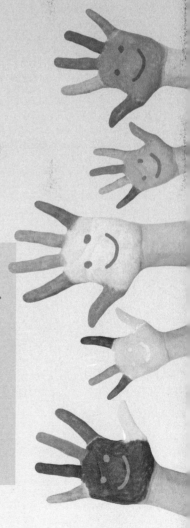

Funny Fingerpainting

Expanding the experience of fingerpainting to whole-hand painting helps students develop the tactile sense they will need for good handwriting.

Preparation: You will need a large sheet of oilcloth, a tarp, or an old shower curtain; paint; masking tape; and fingerpaints. Cover a large table with the oilcloth, and tape down the ends of the oilcloth at the corners of the table.

WHAT TO DO:

1. Drop a blob of paint on the oilcloth in front of each child. Encourage the children to touch the paint, moving it around and making designs on the oilcloth any way they wish.

2. As they explore the paint, ask, "What can you do with this paint using only one finger?" Let them show you.

3. Ask, "Can you paint with your whole hand?" Let them show you what they can do.

4. Encourage them to try painting in different ways and decide which way they like best:
   ○ with one finger
   ○ with more fingers
   ○ with the palm
   ○ with the back of the hand

Let's Paint with Water

While the children will have fun making big random movements, this activity is actually an excellent prewriting activity.

Preparation: You will need water, buckets, wide paintbrushes, and towels.

WHAT TO DO:

1. Take the children outside to a place where they can paint the sides of a building with water. Provide buckets of water and wide paintbrushes.

2. Encourage them to explore putting the water on the wall. Talk with them as they work, noticing details such as, "The brick looks darker when it is wet."

3. Encourage them to use big motions with their brushes. Ask, "Can you paint with very wide strokes from side to side? Can you paint with high strokes from top to bottom? Can you paint in other directions?"

4. Let them paint in any direction they like as long as they are interested.

We Can Paint to the Music

Auditory processing and gross- and fine-motor skills are all part of this artistic experience.

Preparation: You will need several large sheets of paper, tempera paints, paper cups, masking or painter's tape, and paintbrushes. Cover an outside wall with huge sheets of paper. Put tempera paints in a variety of colors in cups for the children. Note: If you decide to do this activity indoors, you will need a drop cloth.

WHAT TO DO:

1. Provide the children with tempera paints and paintbrushes. Encourage them to paint on the paper as big as they can.

2. As they explore the paints, play various types of music, such as classical, hip-hop, techno, lullabies, and marches.

3. From time to time, change the type of music you are playing. Encourage the children to paint in different ways to different music. For example, play a slow lullaby and encourage the children to paint to the gentle tempo. Then, change to a bouncy salsa beat and encourage the children to paint in the way the music makes them feel.

We Can Paint with Our Feet

Use this delightful art activity indoors or out—just be sure to provide a lot of space and time. Get ready for lots of giggles!

Preparation: You will need several aluminum pie pans, washable paint in a variety of colors, buckets of water, towels, and large sheets of oilcloth. Put a different color of paint in each pan. Cover the floor or ground with the oilcloth.

WHAT TO DO:

1. Tell the children that they will each have a chance to choose a color and put their feet in the paint. Then, they will walk across the fabric, making footprints as they go. When they are finished, you will help them step into a bucket of water so they can wash their feet.

2. Ask them to take off their shoes and socks. Let each child, in turn, choose a color and step into a pan.

3. Encourage them to step with their whole foot. What does the imprint look like?

4. Encourage them to tiptoe across the oilcloth, creating designs with their feet.

5. Encourage the children to move any way they like on the oilcloth and then to look at the designs they have made there.

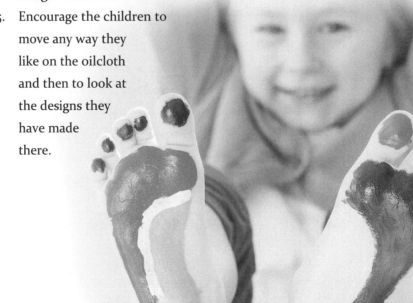

Music

Research suggests a relationship in the brain between music and math from very early ages. Musical elements, such as rhythm, melody, tempo, and beat, share mathematical principles with counting, sequencing, spatial properties, and one-to-one correspondence. Additionally, because music offers experiences shared with others through song, dance, playing, and listening to instruments, there are many opportunities to engage in social-skills learning.

Let's Dance

Every child interprets music in her own way. Children who are observers can choose when to join in.

Preparation: You will need a variety of music, such as classical, jazz, lullabies, and opera.

WHAT TO DO:

1. Play music, and invite the children to dance to it any way they wish.
2. After a while, encourage them to move in different ways, such as the following:
   - hop
   - jump
   - sway
   - slide

3. Vary the rhythm, mood, and genre of the music, giving the children opportunities to dance to fast and slow beats and happy, loud, somber, and quiet music. Encourage them to use their bodies to show if the music is fast or slow, loud or soft, happy or sad.

4. Continue as long as the children are interested, letting them move any way they choose.

Let's Make a Musical Instrument

It is very empowering to make one's own musical instrument. Provide ample opportunities for the children to play their instruments throughout the year.

Preparation: For each child, you will need a small cardboard box with a lid, dry beans in a variety of sizes, and masking tape.

WHAT TO DO:

1. Give each child a box and lid. Ask the children to choose the quantity and size of the beans to put into the box.

2. When they are satisfied with their boxes' contents, let them tape the box tops securely closed. Help them, as needed.

3. Tell them that they will get to play their instruments. Ask, "Can you shake your instruments way up high?" Encourage them to hold the boxes over their heads and shake, shake, shake.

4. Ask, "Can you shake it down low?" Let them show you.

5. Ask them to shake their instruments in a variety of ways:
   ○ under one arm   ○ with two hands
   ○ under the other arm   ○ with one hand
   ○ behind the back

6. Encourage the children to form a line and march, jump, slide, or wiggle around the room, shaking the instruments any way they like.

Let's Move to the Beat

Matching movement to an auditory cue helps children develop rhythm, which can help with self-regulation and more sophisticated mental processing.

Preparation: You will need a drum or rhythm sticks.

WHAT TO DO:

1. Using a drum or rhythm sticks, tap out a slow beat.
2. Ask the children to take a step each time they hear the beat. Let them step in place as you play.
3. Ask them to try stepping to the beat with their eyes closed. Encourage them to listen carefully.
4. Change the tempo. Play a faster beat, and encourage them to step in place to it.
5. Continue, changing the tempo from fast to slow. Encourage the children to step to the beat.
6. For an extra challenge, ask them to jump or hop to the beat.

Listen and Move

Heighten auditory skills, enhance appreciation of music, strengthen spatial awareness, and address self-regulation with this musical activity. Be sure to provide plenty of room to move.

Preparation: You will need two different types of music, such as a rhythmic march and a soft lullaby.

WHAT TO DO:

1. Select two types of music, and invite the children to move. Play a march and a lullaby for younger children. Use as many as four different types of music, depending on the developmental stages of the children.

2. As you play the lullaby, ask, "Can you move all around the room as you listen to this lullaby? Can you move, showing the way the lullaby makes you feel?"

3. As you play the march, ask, "Can you move around the room, showing the way marching music makes you feel?"

4. Divide the class in half. If using three types of music, divide the class into three groups.

5. Assign music to each group. To the march group, say, "This group will move the way marching music makes you feel." To the lullaby group, say, "This group will move the way lullaby music makes you feel."

6. To both groups, say, "When you hear your special music, move all around the room. When your music stops, freeze until you hear your music again."

7. Play one type of music, such as the lullaby. Encourage the lullaby group to move while reminding the march group to freeze.

8. Stop the lullaby and play the march. Encourage the march group to move while reminding the lullaby group to freeze.

9. Continue in this manner, challenging the children to listen for their music and to move when they hear it.

Dramatic Play

Teachers see a strong connection between dramatic play in early childhood and academic-skills development in young children. Dramatic play offers opportunities to develop skills in a variety of curriculum areas: social and emotional, language, physical, and cognitive. Early childhood classrooms have the potential to provide dramatic play settings leading to social and cognitive maturity. Research has shown that dramatic play strongly contributes to children's intellectual development. Prop boxes, music, and full-length mirrors will encourage children to bring their own movements to their activities.

A Day at the Beach

While this activity is full of pretend play, giving a real towel to each child offers opportunities for developing tactile processing and bilateral coordination, which means using both sides of the body at the same time.

Preparation: If possible, provide a real towel for each child.

WHAT TO DO:

1. Ask, "Who can go with me on a pretend trip to the pretend beach?"

2. Ask the children what you will need for your trip. Suggest including pretend bathing suits and pretend sunscreen.

3. Encourage the children to pretend with you as you put on your pretend bathing suits and your pretend sunscreen. "Smear the sunscreen all over your arms, from your wrists to your shoulders. Now put it on your legs. Start at your ankles and slide your hands all the way up to your hips."

4. Invite the children to go swimming in the pretend ocean. Let them show you how they would swim and play in the water.

5. Tell them, "Big waves are coming! Let's jump over the waves or pretend to swim through them."

6. Say, "It's time to come out of the water now. Use your pretend towel to dry yourself off." Dry different body parts:
   - back
   - face
   - shoulders
   - arms
   - one leg at a time

Let's Build a House

Prior to introducing this activity, give the children opportunities to see and safely handle real tools, including hammers, nails, drills, and saws.

Preparation: If possible, bring in examples of real tools for the children to examine, with adult supervision.

WHAT TO DO:

1. Invite the children to build a pretend house with you. Ask, "When we pretend to build a house, what tools do we need?" Let them tell you what you will need. If they are not sure, suggest hammers, nails, drills, and saws.

2. Ask, "Can you show me how to hammer pretend nails?" Let them pretend to hammer, moving their arms up and down.

3. Invite them to pretend to hammer with other parts of their bodies:
   - one foot
   - both feet
   - one elbow
   - bottom
   - tummy

4. Invite the children to use each of the tools you mentioned to build your pretend house.
   - hammer: up and down movements
   - saw: back and forth
   - drill: around and around

Let's Take a Pretend Nature Walk

Before children can imagine a pretend walk, they need to have experienced a real one. Invite them to embellish their actual experiences with pretend ones.

WHAT TO DO:

1. Take the children on a walk outside, drawing their attention to many elements of nature, such as trees, leaves, flowers, and grass.
2. Go back to the classroom, and discuss with them what they saw.
3. Invite the children to go with you on a *pretend* nature walk. Ask, "What would we see on a nature walk?"
4. Pretend to climb up some steep hills, then run down those hills.
5. Pretend to walk carefully on pretend rocks as you cross the pretend river.
6. Tiptoe past the pretend deer so you do not scare them.
7. Stomp past the pretend bears to scare them away.
8. Invite the children to pair up and take turns leading their friends, pretending to take a nature walk.

Let's Take a Trip to a Farm

Prior to taking your pretend farm trip, read several books on farm animals, such as *Barnyard Banter* by Denise Fleming, *Big Red Barn* by Margaret Wise Brown, and *Spot Goes to the Farm* by Eric Hill. Auditory processing enhances the dramatic play of this activity.

WHAT TO DO:

1. Invite the children to join you on a pretend visit to a farm. Ask, "What animals might we see at a farm?" Let the

children name some animals. If they are not sure, suggest cows, horses, pigs, roosters, dogs, cats, and sheep.

2. Encourage them to move like the animals. Let them move around as you call out the names of animals for them to imitate.

3. Ask, "What sounds do those animals make?" Call out the names of the animals and let the children make those animal noises.

4. Tell the children that you will make sounds like different farm animals. When they hear an animal sound, tell them they can move around the classroom like that animal. Comment on their efforts, "Jamie is waddling and flapping his arms like a duck's wings!"

Social Skills

Even though preschoolers are focused on their own needs and desires, they are also curious about the world around them. As you turn their attention from themselves to their immediate families, extended families, neighborhood, and community, they begin taking on the perspective of others. They expand their world of awareness and concern, becoming more competent in their social-emotional development.

Understanding Cues

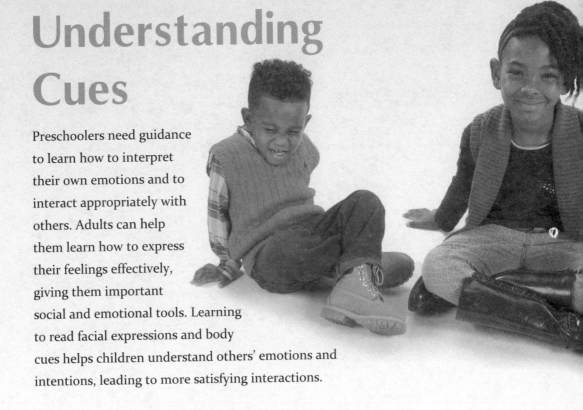

Preschoolers need guidance to learn how to interpret their own emotions and to interact appropriately with others. Adults can help them learn how to express their feelings effectively, giving them important social and emotional tools. Learning to read facial expressions and body cues helps children understand others' emotions and intentions, leading to more satisfying interactions.

Watch My Face

Showing and interpreting emotion with one's whole body develops and enhances empathy.

WHAT TO DO:

1. Discuss different feelings with the children, such as happy, sad, scared, surprised, sleepy, and angry. Ask them how they might know what someone else is feeling.

2. Show them how these feelings look with your facial expressions. Ask, "Can you tell how I'm feeling by looking at my face?" Show a variety of facial expressions, and let them tell you what feelings they recognize.

3. Show them different facial expressions. Encourage the children to use their whole bodies and move around the room as if they are feeling the same way. Let them show you happy, sad, scared, surprised, sleepy, and angry. Comment on their efforts and choices: "Ilana is showing angry feelings by stomping."

Should We Play Together or Alone?

As the children learn to respect each other's personal space, this activity enhances social and spatial awareness while strengthening listening skills.

Preparation: You will need several large, plastic hoops, the same number as there are children participating. Scatter the hoops on the floor around the room. Note: If you do not have enough hoops, you can make large circles on the floor with painter's tape.

WHAT TO DO:

1. Tell the children that you will play some music. When they hear it, they can jump around the room. When the music stops, they should jump inside a hoop and stop.

2. Play music, and let the children jump around.

3. Stop the music, and encourage the children to jump into a hoop and stop.

4. After a few turns, change the game. Say, "When the music stops, I'll say, 'I want to be alone,' or 'Come play with me.' When you hear, 'I want to be alone,' jump into a hoop by yourself. When you hear, 'Come play with me,' jump into a hoop with someone else."

5. Play music, stopping it occasionally. Encourage the children to jump into a hoop alone or with friends depending on what you say when the music stops.

This Is How We Feel

This very subjective fine-motor activity will result in a wide range of emotional representations.

Preparation: You will need crayons and paper for the children.

WHAT TO DO:

1. Give the children a variety of crayons and some paper.

2. Ask them to draw a happy picture. As they work, comment on their choices: "Kim, I see you're drawing a smiling girl and the sun and some flowers." "Matteo, you're drawing a dog. Does your dog make you feel happy?"

3. Ask them to draw a picture of another emotion, such as sad, angry, or surprised. As they work, comment on their choices.

4. Ask them to draw a picture of any feeling they choose.

5. Invite the children to take turns holding up their pictures and letting their classmates guess the feeling the picture is showing.

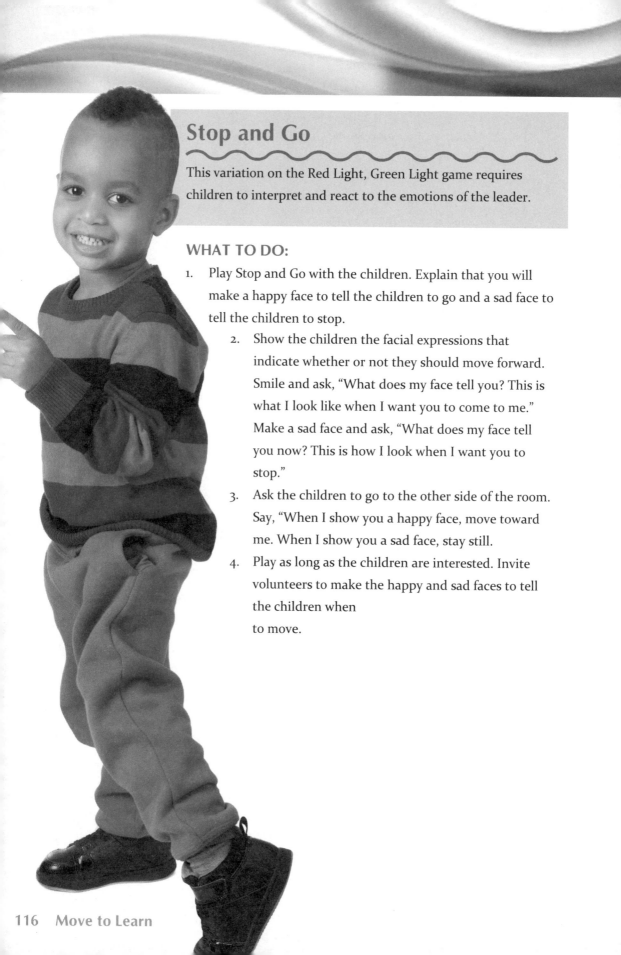

Stop and Go

This variation on the Red Light, Green Light game requires children to interpret and react to the emotions of the leader.

WHAT TO DO:

1. Play Stop and Go with the children. Explain that you will make a happy face to tell the children to go and a sad face to tell the children to stop.

2. Show the children the facial expressions that indicate whether or not they should move forward. Smile and ask, "What does my face tell you? This is what I look like when I want you to come to me." Make a sad face and ask, "What does my face tell you now? This is how I look when I want you to stop."

3. Ask the children to go to the other side of the room. Say, "When I show you a happy face, move toward me. When I show you a sad face, stay still.

4. Play as long as the children are interested. Invite volunteers to make the happy and sad faces to tell the children when to move.

A Sense of Communal Belonging

A safe and welcoming classroom fosters love for learning and a sense of well-being in the learning environment. Being identified as an essential part of a community creates happy and successful learners. Teachers have many opportunities to show respect for each individual and to transmit that attitude. As teachers express concern for all class members and a belief in their abilities to excel, they provide behavior models for all students, other staff members, and families and create a positive learning environment.

What Am I Doing?

Photographs help commemorate special shared experiences. A photo album helps members of a community bond through laughter and shared memories, fostering a sense of belonging.

Preparation: Spend a few weeks taking photos of the children doing different activities and in different groupings. Put the photos together in a class photo album.

WHAT TO DO:

1. Share the photo album with the children.
2. As you look through it, talk about the activities the children are doing in the pictures: "Cynthia, do you remember when you and Michael were climbing on the jungle gym together?"

3. Encourage the children to re-enact what they are doing in the photos. "Cynthia, can you show us how you moved then?" Let her pretend to climb.

4. Continue, showing photos of each child and encouraging the children to re-enact the movements they are doing in the photos.

Let's Play Hoop Group

While playing this terrific cooperation game, prepare to hear loads of giggles as the children fit—and eventually cram—themselves into the hoops.

Preparation: You will need one large plastic hoop per child. Place the hoops on the floor throughout the classroom.

WHAT TO DO:

1. Ask the children to stand inside a hoop. There should be one child in each hoop.

2. Tell them you will play music, and encourage the children to move around the room as you do. Tell them that, when the music stops, they can quickly jump into the hoops.

3. Play the music and let the children move around, then stop it and let them jump into a hoop.

4. Each time the music starts, ask the children to move in different ways, such as the following:
   ○ Move around the room way up high.
   ○ Move around way down low.
   ○ Move around on your bottom.
   ○ Move around on your tummy.

5. Keep playing the game, and as the music plays, remove one hoop. Now, some of the children will have to share hoops. Tell them, "You might need to share a hoop with a friend. Make sure all of the hoops have at least one person inside."

6. Start the music again, and as the children move to it, remove another hoop.

7. Continue playing, removing one hoop each time the music starts. This activity ends when there are only two hoops remaining and all the children are standing in one or the other hoop.

Let's Make a Class Picture

Children three-and-a-half years old and older can acquire an appreciation of each group member as they all contribute to the completion of a single project.

Preparation: You will need several markers and a very large piece of paper—at least three square feet.

WHAT TO DO:

1. Ask the children to sit in a circle, and explain that you need them to help you make a picture of everyone in the class. Tell them that they will be invited to work on the picture during free-choice activity time as you call their names when it is time for them to help.

2. Invite the children to choose centers where they can spend the next forty-five minutes interacting with friends and materials.

3. During that period, ask three children to hop, jump, march, or slither to you. Invite them to create a picture of themselves with markers on the big paper. Write the child's name under his likeness. When the children have completed their pictures, invite three more children to draw themselves.

4. When every child has had an opportunity to draw a picture of himself, bring the class together to sit in a circle. Show them the picture, and ask them to take turns explaining their drawings.

5. After everyone has had an opportunity to speak, hang the picture on a wall or bulletin board at the children's eye level. Above the picture, hang a sign that says, "All of the people in our class." Let the children know that they can admire the picture any time they wish.

6. Be sure to invite children who were absent from class during this activity to draw their pictures when they return.

This Is Our Friendship Snack

Helping children appreciate the importance of tasting new items encourages them to accept others' food choices.

Preparation: Find a number of healthy, easy recipes that are representative of the cultures of the children in your class. Ask parents for their easy recipes or guidance in preparation of the snack. Purchase ingredients, and prepare the snack in the classroom, if possible. Be aware of your center's allergy policies.

WHAT TO DO:

1. Each week, feature a different ethnic snack. While also offering regular classroom snack choices and being cognizant of food allergies, encourage the children to sample the new foods.

2. Talk about the new snack: "Melissa, your mom told me that you like to eat this snack (name the food) at home. What do you like about it? Do you think it is smooth or crunchy or chewy or soft?" Ask the children for their opinions: "What do other people think about the snack?" Listen to the children's responses.

3. Say, "Next week, we will try another kind of snack, one that Marco's family likes to eat. After we taste it, we'll decide if it is smooth, crunchy, chewy, or soft."

4. When the snack is finished, ask the children to move to the trash can in different ways. Say, "Think about whether Melissa's snack was smooth, crunchy, chewy, or soft. I will ask you to move to the trash can in different ways for each of the things you think about the snack."

   ○ If you think the snack was smooth, slide to throw your trash away.

   ○ If you think it was chewy, jump as you throw your trash away.

   ○ If it was crunchy, hop on one foot to the trash can.

   ○ If it was soft, wiggle to get to the trash can.

   "We'll have more chances to move those ways after eating Marco's snack next week."

Cooperation

Early childhood educators are in a position to foster cooperation in their classrooms in a variety of ways. They can encourage children and adults to communicate respectfully by listening and speaking in turn. They can include children with diverse needs and skills in cooperative play and work activities. They can play cooperative games rather than competitive games. They can use the word *cooperate* in classroom discussions, clearly defining and celebrating the children's cooperative behaviors.

Who Is the Cooperation Helper for Today?

With an emphasis on mindfulness and with the assistance of an adult, four-year-olds can focus on the needs of others. This activity contributes to the development of self-control and an appreciation of each other, as every child has an opportunity to help classmates cooperate.

WHAT TO DO:

1. Talk with the children about cooperating. Explain what it means to cooperate, and let the children tell you their ideas for how they can cooperate with their classmates and with you.

2. Give everyone who wishes to participate an opportunity to serve as a cooperation helper. Each day, assign someone the role of cooperation helper for the day. Encourage that child to help others find ways to cooperate.

3. Ask the cooperation helper to intercede when children are having trouble getting along. For example, if two children are not sharing toys, ask, "Anthony and Ari, do you need help figuring out how to share the toys? Would you like for

today's cooperation helper to help you remember how to do that? Gretchen, you're the cooperation helper for today. Can you help us figure out how to share the toys?" Let her offer ideas (with your help), such as letting each boy choose a toy, take turns with a favorite toy, or take turns in a play area.

4. Tell the children that you will know that they have solved the problem when you see them jumping. Say, "Let's remember that we use words to help us cooperate. I'll know when this problem has been taken care of when I see the three of you jumping."

5. Tell the children, "Tomorrow, someone else will be the cooperation helper." Everyone will have a chance to do it for one day.

Moving with My Friend

Besides offering a fun way to address cooperation, this activity helps develop body awareness and proprioception.

Preparation: You will need one beanbag for each pair of children.

WHAT TO DO:

1. Ask the children to choose partners. Give each pair a beanbag.

2. Ask a pair of children to hold their beanbag up without using their hands and to show how they can move together around the room without dropping the beanbag.

3. As they move around the room, comment on their choices: "Daniel and Gabrielle, you are walking while holding the beanbag with your hips. You are really cooperating to hold the beanbag."

4. Encourage other pairs of children to hold the beanbag in different ways as they move around the room, such as the following:

- ○ with their elbows
- ○ with their hips
- ○ with their heads
- ○ with their shoulders
- ○ with their backs

5. Comment on their choices for how to hold the beanbags and on their ability to cooperate.

Jump over the Rope

As the children move from one side of the room to the other, going over or under a rope, they are enhancing their spatial awareness, body awareness, and directionality.

Preparation: You will need a rope at least ten feet in length. If the class is large, you may need a longer rope so that everyone has space to move.

WHAT TO DO:

1. Invite two volunteers to take either end of the rope. Ask them to stretch the rope out as far as it will go and then sit down on the floor while holding the rope.
2. Encourage the other children to take turns jumping over the rope.
3. Ask the rope-holders to raise the rope a little. Encourage the children to jump over the rope again.
4. Continue the game, asking the holders to move the rope in different ways for the children to jump over:
    - ○ lower the rope
    - ○ shake the rope
    - ○ wiggle the rope

    Encourage the children to find a way to go over the rope without stepping on it.
5. Ask the children to pair up and continue the game.

Let's Play Kids' Obstacle Course

This is a wonderful activity to use when parents come to visit the classroom. The parents can be obstacles, and the children can navigate through the course.

WHAT TO DO:

1. Tell the children that they will make a Kids' Obstacle Course with their own bodies. Encourage them to think of ways to form an obstacle that their friends have to go over, under, between, or around.

2. Divide the class in half. Ask one half to sit down.

3. Ask the children in the other half to pair up.

4. Ask some of the pairs to form an obstacle that their friends will have to go under, some to form an obstacle that their friends will go over, some an obstacle that their friends will go between, and some an obstacle that their friends will go around. When they become the obstacle, ask them to hold that pose.

5. Encourage the sitting half to take turns navigating the Kids' Obstacle Course. Help them move through each obstacle, including over, under, around, and between.

6. When all of the children have moved through the obstacle course, switch and let the "obstacle" group be the ones who navigate the other group's Kids' Obstacle Course.

Appendix
CREATIVE MOVEMENT
TEMPLATE

(Adapted from *In-Sync Activity Cards* by Joye Newman and Carol Kranowitz.)

When planning a creative movement lesson, please consider the following components:

- **Time:** Are the children moving quickly, slowly, or somehow in-between?
- **Level:** Are the children moving way up high, way down low, or in-between?
- **Quality:** Are the children moving gently or heavily?
- **Pathway:** Are the children moving on a straight line or a curved one?
- **Direction:** Are the children moving forward, backward, or in some other direction?

Once you choose your movement, changing any one of these components will offer the children the opportunity to think and plan as they move.

Here are some suggestions:

Movement	Time	Level	Quality	Pathway	Direction
Walking	Fast	Way up high	Gently	Straight	Forward
Jumping	Slow	Way down low	Loudly	Curved	Backward
Marching	Medium	Medium	Happily	Zigzag	Toward a target
Sliding			Angrily	Spiral	Diagonally

References

Bobbio, Tatiana, Carl Gabbard, and Priscila Cacola. 2009. "Interlimb Coordination: An Important Facet of Gross-Motor Ability." *Early Childhood Research and Practice* 11(2).

Burack, Jodi. 2005. "Uniting Mind and Music: Shaw's Vision Continues." *American Music Teacher* 55(1): 84–87.

Chenfeld, Mimi Brodsky. 2004. "Education Is a Moving Experience: Get Movin'." *Young Children* 59(4): 56–59.

Diamond, Adele. 2000. "Close Interrelation of Motor Development and Cognitive Development and of the Cerebellum and Prefrontal Cortex." *Child Development* 71(1): 44–56.

Gabbard, Carl. 2008. *Lifelong Motor Development*, 5th ed. San Francisco: Pearson.

Geist, Kamile, Eugene Geist, and Kathleen Kuznik. 2012. "The Patterns of Music: Young Children Learning Mathematics Through Beat, Rhythm, and Melody." *Young Children* 67(1): 74–79.

Greenough, William, and James Black. 1992. "Induction of Brain Structure by Experience: Substrates for Cognitive Development. In *Minnesota Symposia on Child Psychology: Developmental Behavioral Neuroscience* 24. Hillsdale, NJ: Lawrence Erlbaum.

Jensen, Eric. 2005. *Teaching with the Brain in Mind*, 2nd ed. Alexandria, VA: Association for Supervision and Curriculum Development.

Kranowitz, Carol. 2006. *The Out-of-Sync Child Has Fun: Activities for Kids with Sensory Processing Disorder*. New York: Penguin.

Kranowitz, Carol, and Joye Newman. 2010. *Growing an In-Sync Child: Simple, Fun Activities to Help Every Child Develop, Learn, and Grow*. New York: Penguin.

Newman, Joye, and Carol Kranowitz. 2011. *In-Sync Activity Cards: 50 Simple, New Activities to Help Children Develop, Learn, and Grow!* Arlington, TX: Sensory World.

Piaget, Jean. 1962. *Play, Dreams, and Imitation in Childhood*. New York: Norton.

Shatz, Carla. 1992. "The Developing Brain." *Scientific American*. Special issue: 3–9.

Smilansky, Sara, and Leah Shefatya. 1990. *Facilitating Play: A Medium for Promoting Cognitive, Socio-Emotional, and Academic Development in Young Children*. Gaithersburg, MD: Psychological and Educational Publications.

Wu, Tao, Kenji Kansaku, and Mark Hallett. 2004. "How Self-Initiated Memorized Movements Become Automatic: A Functional MRI Study." *Journal of Neurophysiology* 91(4): 1690–1698.

Zull, James. 2004. "The Art of Changing the Brain." *Educational Leadership* 62(1): 68–72.

Suggested Readings

Children's Books

Brown, Margaret Wise. 1947. *Goodnight Moon.* New York: HarperCollins.

Keats, Ezra Jack. 1962. *The Snowy Day.* New York: Viking Juvenile.

Seuss, Dr. 1960. *Oh, the Places You'll Go!* New York: Random House.

Slobodkina, Esphyr. 1938. *Caps for Sale: A Tale of a Peddler, Some Monkeys, and Their Monkey Business.* New York: HarperCollins.

Books for Professionals

Boyd, Kassandra, Melanie Chalk, and Jennifer Law. 2003. *Kids on the Move: Creative Movement for Children of All Ages.* College Station, TX: Creative Publishing.

Brehm, Madeleine, and Nancy Tindell. 1983. *Movement with a Purpose: Perceptual Motor-Lesson Plans for Young Children.* West Nyack, NY: Parker.

Carlson, Frances. 2011. *Big Body Play: Why Boisterous, Vigorous, and Very Physical Play Is Essential to Children's Development and Learning.* Washington, DC: National Association for the Education of Young Children.

Dow, Connie. 2006. *Dance, Turn, Hop, Learn! Enriching Movement Activities for Preschoolers.* St. Paul, MN: Redleaf.

Kranowitz, Carol. 2006. *The Out-of-Sync Child Has Fun: Activities for Kids with Sensory Processing Disorder.* New York: Penguin.

Kranowitz, Carol, and Joye Newman. 2010. *Growing an In-Sync Child: Simple, Fun Activities to Help Every Child Develop, Learn, and Grow.* New York: Penguin.

Landy, Joanne, and Keith Burridge. 2000. *Fundamental Motor Skills and Movement Activities for Young Children.* St. Paul, MN: Center for Applied Research in Education.

Newman, Joye, and Carol Kranowitz. 2011. *In-Sync Activity Cards: 50 Simple, New Activities to Help Children Develop, Learn, and Grow!* Arlington, TX: Sensory World.

Smith, Jodene. 2004. *Activities for Gross Motor Skills Development.* Westminster, CA: Teacher Created Resources.

Stinson, Bill. 1990. *Moving and Learning for the Young Child.* Reston, VA: American Alliance for Health, Physical Education, Recreation, and Dance.

Thompson, Myra. 1993. *Jump for Joy! Over 375 Creative Movement Activities for Young Children.* Saddle River, NJ: Prentice Hall.

Torbert, Marianne. 1980. *Follow Me: A Handbook of Movement Activities for Children.* Upper Saddle River, NJ: Prentice Hall.

Torbert, Marianne, and Lynne Schneider. 1993. *Follow Me Too: A Handbook of Movement Activities for Three-to-Five-Year-Olds.* Menlo Park, CA: Addison-Wesley.

Index